A SONG OF CREATION

A SONG OF CREATION

Selections from  The First Article

H. Boone Porter

COWLEY

Published in the United States of America
by Cowley Publications and Forward Movement Publications.

Typesetting by Burnes Associates.

International Standard Book Number: 0-936384-34-4

Library of Congress Cataloging-in-Publication Data

Porter, Harry Boone, 1923–
   A song of creation.

   1. Creation--Meditations.   I. Title.
BT695.P67 1986   231.7'65   86-6285
ISBN 0-936384-34-4 (pbk.)

Published in the United States of America by
Cowley Publications
980 Memorial Drive
Cambridge, MA 02138
Forward Movement Publications
412 Sycamore Street
Cincinnati, OH 45202

To Clarissa
who shared
many of these times and places

CONTENTS

1. WHAT WE START WITH   1
      What We Start With   3
      The Pot that Came to Life   5
      In the Image of God   7
      Breath of Life   10
      Shared Universe   12
      Partnership in Creation   14
      Labor and Leisure   18
      Evolution and Fundamentalism   22
      Eagles, Skunks, and Tapirs   26
      The New Creation   29

2. PRUNING THE APPLE TREE   33
      Deep Cold   35
      On the Ice   37
      Pruning the Apple Tree   40
      Old Man River   43
      Cow Parsnips and the Tree of Life   45
      Animals Seen and Unseen   47
      As the Sand on the Seashore   50

Haymaking at Sunset   53
Cold Water   55
Field of Corn   58
Down in the Briar Patch   60
Autumn Mist   63

3. SUMMER NIGHTS   65
Moon Time   67
Sabbath Time   69
The Sun Coming Forth   73
Summer Nights   75
The Night of Life   78
The Meaning of Blackness   80
The Circle of Past and Future   82
Getting Ready   85
Incarnation and Light   87
The Watches of the Night   90
Eve and Mary   93

4. SEEING CREATION   97
Seeing Creation   99
Yes and No   101
The Fireplace in Lent   104
Gardener's Prime Time   107
Saint's Day on Saturday   111
Barefoot on the Path of Life   113
Led by Our Noses   116
Berchtesgaden   118
Law and Life   121
An Ethic of Creation   123
Natural Theology   126
Spirituality and Creation   129

Introduction

Does the natural world around us, of which we are a part, have meaning and purpose? Is it only a vast impersonal machine, which originated at some time by sheer accident? Or does it express beauty, love, and spiritual value? The essays in this book represent efforts to answer these questions through observing the world about us in aspects of daily life which we often ignore. These questions, directly or indirectly, face all of us. For many, an appreciation of the wonder of the universe and the flowering of life within it is the starting point of our spiritual pilgrimage. The meaning of the world is inevitably a religious question.

The link between the natural world and the realm of spiritual values has historically been, for Christians, Jews, and Moslems, the doctrine of creation, the conviction that the one good and loving God created the universe. In our own time, the very word "creation" has become a bone of contention. On the one hand, it has been upheld by those who demand a highly literal interpretation of the biblical story of creation and who deny scientific views of the emergence of life on this planet. Conversely, a narrow view of natural science has inculcated disregard for the spiritual message the biblical story was intended to convey. The creationism controversy has been fought at a crude level. Yet the problem of reconciling the world of the natural sciences with the world of value, meaning, and spiritual

significance remains as the single most challenging intellectual
task of our era.

Because of both the urgency and the fascination of these
questions, in 1978 I began for *The Living Church* a weekly
column of essays entitled "The First Article." The reference
was not really to the fact that this column came at the
beginning of the magazine, but rather to the belief in one
God, creator of heaven and earth, traditionally known as the
first article of the Christian Faith. It appears at the beginning
of the Apostles' and the Nicene Creed, at the beginning of
the Bible, and implicitly at the beginning of the Lord's
Prayer. It is a good place to begin, a good place to begin again
if we have lost our way, and a good place to return to in our
own spiritual journey.

From 1970 to 1977 I lived with my family on a church-
owned farm named Roanridge outside of Kansas City,
Missouri. Those years are reflected in some of these essays.
At that time the American Book of Common Prayer was
being revised. One of the fundamental questions to be considered was whether Christian worship was to continue to be
grounded, as it had been for so many centuries, in the natural
world and its cycle of seedtime and harvest, or whether it was
to be primarily reflective of the human thoughts and experiences of our modern mechanized and commercialized life.
I came down strongly for the former and urged the inclusion
of the many references to creation in the liturgy, believing
that access to the deeper and older springs of life is one of
the invaluable contributions that liturgy can make to human
life in our day. It is part of the historic and Catholic heritage
of Christianity which many modern people have lost.

More recently we have resided in Southern Wisconsin,
first in a house on Pine Lake, a beautiful body of water in
Waukesha County, and subsequently on a small and somewhat dilapidated farm in Dodge County through which the

little Ashippun River flows. Some of these areas are reflected
in the essays gathered here, as are summertime visits to
Cuttyhunk, a small island off the coast of southern Massachu-
setts where many parts of this book were written or revised.

I wish to express my gratitude to many who have contributed to this book in a variety of ways, particularly to my
wife Violet who has constantly urged me on. I appreciate the
interest of many readers whose encouragement has meant
much. I am grateful to the editor of the Cowley Press,
Cynthia Shattuck, for her patient attention to the manuscript
over a long period.

1. What We Start With

O all ye works of the Lord, bless ye the Lord;
　praise him and magnify him for ever.
O ye angels of the Lord, bless ye the Lord;
　praise him and magnify him for ever.

What We Start With

Our createdness is what we start with, our beginning. We are, therefore, we think, feel, and act in a variety of ways. How we came to be here, and what it means for us to be here is a never-ending topic of reflection. The entrance of human life into this world is the subject of an almost limitless variety of stories, myths, legends, and epics. One particular account has had a unique impact on the thought and imagination of Western civilization. It is the account given in the opening pages of the Bible, in the Book of Genesis.

This ancient account of creation may easily be misunderstood in a wooden manner, simply as an inventory of divine accomplishments on a particular working week. More helpfully, it can be understood as a mysterious tale which awakens in the perceptive reader an awareness of the vastness, beauty, and wonder of the universe, an epic which always raises more questions than it answers, a constant challenge to us to enter personally and consciously into the meaning of the universe of which we are a part.

If we accept the invitation to ponder on the ancient words of the first two or three pages of our Bible, we find various ways that we can appropriate for ourselves what it has to say. We can, as it were, verify it by discovering within our own daily existence that life is indeed a gift, reflecting the power, the wisdom, and the love of the Giver. Our own eyes can discover new things in human life, in the life of other creatures, and indeed in the inanimate physical stuff which is, quite literally, the ground on which earthly life rests.

Things become different. Many metaphors and figures of speech have been used again and again to describe this kind of difference. It is like going along a path and then turning a corner and seeing a new and unexpected prospect before one. It is like crossing a body of water and finding a new place on the other side. It is like being in the dark and suddenly having a light. It is like opening a book and finding a new realm of life and thought within it. It is like opening a gate into a garden.

To discover our createdness, to discover that we were made and are upheld by an infinitely wise and loving God, can be all of this. This is, in a sense, what the biblical story of creation is saying. It faces us as we open the beginning of a mysterious and fascinating book. It begins by telling of darkness being replaced by light. It tells us of a garden. And it may be a long long journey for us to get there, or to return there, to discover how far it is, or how close it is.

This journey is life itself. Its destination is somehow its starting point: where it began is its goal. Yet each glimpse of our destination shows it new. After millions of years, the world God made still unfolds itself as new. Our lives can be new, we can be new. This is all part, a very small part, of what creation is.

Everything we touch, see, hear, smell, or taste is part of God's created world, though few people perceive it as such. We give to each its proper honor when we see it in terms of its createdness, when we recognize it as something made by God. Piece by piece, we begin to realize what an astonishing place God has put us in. We discover that we are citizens of a universe more wonderful than we ever could have imagined. Yet even so, as the Book of Ecclesiasticus says, "we have seen but few of his works" (43: 32).

The Pot that Came to Life

The first chapter of the first book of the Bible expresses the concept of creation in different ways and at different levels. The beginning of a day, the beginning of a week, and the beginning of a year are ingeniously woven in together.

The second chapter of Genesis gives a somewhat different account of creation, but it also speaks of a variety of beginnings. Most notably, it tells of the beginning of man. The first chapter had the brief but noble statement that humans, man and woman, are created in the image and likeness of God (verses 26 and 27). The second chapter, on the other hand, has a longer and literally earthier tale, animated by a certain whimsical humor and shrewd insight. Here the earth is first like a bare, dry field (verse 5). Then God moistens it. Taking some clay, he proceeds to mold it into a vessel. When he is finished, he blows into the snout of it and it becomes alive—to the delight, but later to the grief, of its Creator! He gives this creature a garden in which to live. Then God makes him a zoo of live toys with which to amuse himself, while God (like a proud parent standing hidden back of a Christmas tree) listens to hear the noises the youngster makes and the names he gives to things. Not content with this, God makes him a sister to be his companion and to fill out the family.

We cannot really understand the second chapter of Genesis if we think it is a scientific treatise, or a philosophic disquisition. It is a vivid and touching story, a story very much like *Pinocchio*, for instance, or *The Gingerbread Man*. One has to see both the humor and the pathos to perceive what this story is communicating. Humor and pathos are both about the irony of life, the good-in-badness and bad-in-goodness of human existence. This is what it is about. It is this unique quality of human life, dividing us so sharply from animals, that is being expressed.

So in this second chapter humans come upon the scene—a boy and a girl, naked oriental children. They soon grow up, have an altercation with their heavenly Father, and set out to homestead for themselves, with all the joys and sorrows of working and raising their own family. It is, in a sense, the life of the typical man and woman.

The second chapter of Genesis presents the doctrine of creation, the first article of our faith, in terms of a human life. You were made by God; I was made by God; everyone was made by God. Yet we only become fully ourselves, fully what he intends us to be, when we know that this is so. The Bible asks us to recognize that we are, after all, odd-looking pieces of pottery. On the other hand, we are molded by God himself, he has breathed into us, and it is he who loves us. It is on these terms that we are called to live with ourselves, with one another, and with God.

In the Image of God

The first chapter of the Bible puts before us the creation of all living things. Life is of astonishing variety, in the water, on land, and in the air. The shapes of animals, their habits, needs, and ways of meeting their needs, and the relation of animals to plants, represent an almost endless series of balanced combinations. In some ways, modern biological science has given us more knowledge of this than people ever had before. On the other hand, more primitive folk, living close to nature, had an intimate and firsthand awareness of it which we lack. Of course the 31 verses of Genesis 1 do not undertake to describe the whole of animal or plant life: they seek rather to suggest it, to remind us of it, to bring before the eyes of our mind the wonder, the richness, and the beauty of living things.

Amidst all the animate creatures, so diverse in size, shape, color, and gait, one kind is different. The man and woman cannot run so fast as other long-legged animals. They are weaker than animals half their size. Their teeth and claws are pathetic as weapons. Unlike their furry neighbors, they are naked. Yet they alone, as they stand up conspicuously, with their eyes focused ahead, and their hands free to seize, shape, mold, and use what they encounter—they alone, the man and the woman, look like God.

That is indeed a conversation stopper. What can one say next? This amazing idea at the beginning of the Bible (v. 27) is one to ponder: we and our ancestors have been pondering it for thousands of years.

7

Of course people look like other things too. We are like
animated pots, the second chapter of Genesis humorously suggests. We are rather closely related to apes, as anyone who
has recently been to a zoo has probably noticed. People have
been compared to trees, rocks, and so forth. But the serious
thing is that in some sense or other we were made in the
image and likeness of God. To understand about human
beings, you have to know that.

One way to deal with this is to explore the abstract and
theoretical senses of the words image and likeness. Perhaps
image means one thing and likeness means something else.
Perhaps they refer to the creative powers which we, in some
humble way, share with God. Perhaps they refer to power
over other animals. Perhaps they refer to our reason, our
conceptualizing and rational minds, or our powers to make
moral judgments and choices—in other words, our freedom.
Philosophers and theologians have expounded all these pos-
sibilities.

To some extent no doubt all these interpretations contain
truths, although let us not forget that our inner and outer
selves are very closely related. Our minds developed as they
did in part at least because we have stereoscopic vision,
because our mouths (unimpaired by fangs) can articulate
complicated audible signals, and because our hands can man-
ipulate what is around us. Perhaps this is suggested and
poetically alluded to in the brief lines of Genesis. Certainly
the Hebrews had a very unified view of human beings as
animated creatures, with body and soul closely tied together.

Yet we return to the story of creation and encounter the
idea that in the first instance, at the simplest level, it means
that the man and the woman somehow looked like God—
embarrassing, puzzling, or frightening as that may be. All
animals reflect the Creator's power and wisdom. All in some

way give evidence of his greatness and glory. Yet the man and woman alone have a personal similarity to him.

This is rather like those old-fashioned stories in which a ragged waif is suddenly recognized as looking like the king, and so is discovered to be the long lost prince. Or like Cinderella, the dirty girl who cleans the fireplace, who is recognized as the sweetheart of the great lord. Although we are covered with a dirt worse than ashes, although it will take many an ordeal to bring us back home, God calls you and me to the discovery that we, even we ourselves, are to be made heirs of the kingdom. He has recognized us even though we have not recognized ourselves or one another.

"Therefore it says 'Awake, thou that sleepest, and arise from the dead, and Christ shall give thee light' " (Eph. 5:14).

Breath of Life

Whitsunday or Pentecost calls our attention to the last part of both the Nicene and the Apostles' Creeds—to our affirmation of belief regarding the Holy Spirit, the holy church, the forgiveness of sins and the resurrection to eternal life. The doctrine of creation, on the other hand, stands in the first article of our belief, at the very beginning of the creeds. Pentecost and creation thus appear at first glance to be at opposite ends of the Christian outlook.

It may seem paradoxical that Psalm 104, the great psalm of creation, should provide the first choice of psalmody for this feast in the Book of Common Prayer. In previous editions of the Prayer Book this same psalm is part of the proper for this feast (at Evensong), right back to the middle of the 16th century.

Certainly the association of this psalm with this day is partly attributable to verse 31: "You send forth your Spirit, and they [all living things] are created; and so you renew the face of the earth." This verse alone specifically refers to "your Spirit," but it does not stand apart from the meaning of the psalm as a whole. Earlier editions of the Prayer Book number this as verse 30, and translate "your Spirit" as "thy breath."

It is the same thing in the original Hebrew, in which the word *ruach* means both breath and spirit, as is the case also with some other languages. God's breath is the breath of life. It can be as gentle as the quiet respiration of a sleeping baby, or as powerful as "the rush of a mighty wind," which the apostles heard on Pentecost, or as mysterious as the invisible wind of which our Lord speaks to Nicodemus (John 3:8).

The verse referred to in Psalm 104 suggests that as this divine breath conferred life on Adam (Genesis 2:7), so too, in some sense, the Holy Spirit has conferred life on everything which is living. The deity who inspired the apostles on Pentecost was not an obscure little god of Palestine, but rather the God who is God, the God of the whole universe. The calling and destiny of the holy catholic church is in the hands of the Maker of heaven and earth.

There is a wonderful circularity to the creeds or, as we prefer, "the creed," since both formularies express the one faith. We say the latter parts in the light of what has been said before, but the next time we say the creed, we begin our affirmation of God the creator in the light of what has been previously said at the conclusion.

As people who are sanctified by the Holy Spirit and members of the holy church, we go back to affirm our faith in our creator differently. We see God's presence and power where it was invisible before. The natural world, the whole real world of living things, becomes again identifiable as God's garden, and the garden becomes the pathway to the church.

The diversity, beauty, and wonder of all living things also points here (just as it does in the first chapter of Genesis) to the mystery of the new creation of which Christ is the first-born and in which, having been spiritually fruitful in our generation, we will, as Bishop Wordsworth put it in a familiar Easter hymn, ". . . by angel hands be gathered/And be ever, Lord, with thee."

Shared Universe

Theologians and natural scientists have often disagreed about their perceptions of the world around us, and there is the sad record of each group persecuting the other at certain points in history. Yet there is a mysterious and apparently undivorceable marriage between historic Christianity and natural science as it has developed in the Western world during the past several centuries.

Classical Christian theology, the sort of theology Anglican thinkers have generally professed and which is broadly described as catholic, sees human beings as inhabitants of a "universe." The word literally means "one turning"—a unity, something cohesive, the parts of which somehow move together. This is in contrast with the many forms of paganism in which different gods are believed to control different parts of the world. The polytheist, or worshiper of many gods, inhabits not a *universe* but a *multiverse*.

Christianity also stands in contrast to those primitive religions in which a tribal god or gods ruled the affairs of one people in one place, but in which the concept of one God ruling all peoples and all places is lacking. Christianity insists on the wide horizons of the whole world.

It is only within the universe, within a unified and coherent system of reality, that natural science as we know it can develop. The overwhelming consistency of nature's laws and the occurrence of order everywhere are assumptions without which our sort of science could not exist.

The same sense of consistency and order are part of the Christian spiritual outlook. Although this awareness was not reached overnight, Christianity has had to maintain that peoples who live on different sides of the world, and who look physically different, are eligible for salvation on the basis of the same Gospel. Should rational and morally responsible beings be discovered on another planet, they too would be entitled to our respect, and we would have to consider how the truths of the one God applied to them.

The fascination of the planetary novels of C.S. Lewis lies in the convincing presentation of how the truths of Christianity might apply to different kinds of creatures living in utterly different circumstances. The "truth" of such novels is not, of course, in the utterly fictitious scenes and events, but in the coherence with which Christian values are expressed in a wide variety of imaginable situations.

This perhaps sheds light on what may be called the truth of music. Within a particular situation, in this case, within a particular combination of sounds, further sounds are made in accordance with a coherent and orderly pattern. Random notes are not music, just as random events are not a novel, and random facts are not science.

Christian theology and natural science, in spite of disagreements and differences of approach and many historic conflicts, are both irreversibly marked by this investment in the universe, the unified, coherent, orderly cosmos created by the one and only universal and eternal God.

Partnership in Creation

We observe Labor Day by not laboring. This in itself is a vivid example of the paradox of work and play, labor and leisure. We can easily speak, in broad and general terms, of the difference between work time and free time, yet when we try to be very specific, and to draw a sharp line between the two, it is not easy.

Near where I live, two men were recently cutting up the limbs of some trees. It was their work. They evidently did not enjoy it too much and they frequently sat down to rest. I would have had to rest even more, and yet when I chop wood it is a recreational activity, a form of exercise I do enjoy. Some people spend holidays doing things that are much harder—scaling mountains, canoeing down dangerous rivers, or running in marathon races. How much would one have to pay in order to hire people to do such things?

One person's work is another's play. How true this is! Perhaps because the relation between them is so complex and so puzzling, people are always trying to fence off the one from the other. Work areas are in special parts of towns, often walled off, fenced off, or marked by no trespassing signs. When workmen have to do something in an ordinary non-work area, everyone seems to feel better if they divide themselves off with saw-horses. Space to play is also frequently located in special areas, also marked off by walls, fences, and no trespassing signs!

Work is a very peculiar thing, and we use the word itself

with all sorts of special inflections, connotations, and nuances. A suburban householder says he is going to repair his garage roof "after work." This may be a much more difficult and laborious task than anything he has done at his office during the day. A "non-stipendiary farmer" who works eight hours a day at a nearby factory may do his farm chores "before work"—again the former may be more laborious than the latter. Conversely a college professor may complain that her hours of teaching "interfere with her work." For her, the real work is not the teaching she is paid to do, but the research and writing she desires and chooses to do in her free time. Parishioners are sometimes surprised to be told that their rector is "working on his sermon" when they have seen that he is reading a book or going for a walk— yet these may in fact be the ways he can best accomplish this particular work. A woman who devotes her time to household and family responsibilities may be described as a "hard worker," but may also say that she "does not work."

Most forms of what we call work not only take place in prescribed areas, but are surrounded by special conditions and circumstances. Every kind of work tends to have a certain *mystique* of its own. One is usually supposed to be a *member*, a duly admitted participant, in the working group. This may mean being a migrant agricultural worker, or a member of the labor union, or a licensed physician, or a member of the bar, or a recognized artisan. Many forms of work also have their special mannerisms, their own gestures, forms, and ceremonies. The ordinary person may not understand all of their words and may be puzzled or irritated by some of the ways in which they do things, but we would not have confidence in such people or be impressed by them if they did not each have their own recognized professional manner.

We may laugh at occupational or professional foibles and affectations. Yet let us not laugh too hard. In all these ways, men and women are struggling for dignity, credibility, and respect as they go about a multitude of tasks, some of which are exciting and gratifying, and some of which are tedious and discouraging. This is the paradox of work—that it is necessary, honorable, and approved by God, yet so often onerous, painful, and even degrading. The first two chapters of Genesis depicted the role of the man and woman in the garden as one of honor and glory. To till the ground (Genesis 2:5) is apparently to be in partnership with God in his work of creation. In the third chapter, after the fall, the same work appears as a curse and punishment (Genesis 3:17-19). This paradox, the privilege and the burden of work, is what the sons and daughters of Adam and Eve have to deal with.

The Book of the Wisdom of Jesus the Son of Sirach, called Ecclesiasticus (not to be confused with Ecclesiastes), is one of the so-called Apocryphal or Intertestamental Books which appear between the Old and New Testaments in a complete and proper Bible. Chapter 38 includes a long and vivid discussion of different kinds of craftsmen and artisans. The author concludes,

Without them a city cannot be established,
     and men can neither sojourn nor live there. . .
They do not sit in the judge's seat,
     nor do they understand the sentence of judgment;
they cannot expound discipline or judgment,
     and they are not found using proverbs.
But they keep stable the fabric of the world,
     and their prayer is in the practice of their trade.
                                        (Ecclesiasticus 38:32-34)
The final point is a distinctive idea of Judaism and Chris-

tianity. Honest work, whether we feel it a privilege or a curse, whether it be honored or despised, may be offered by the worker as a prayer to God.

Labor and Leisure

We have been talking about a distinctive aspect of our created life in this world, namely work and play, leisure and labor. The topic is hardly unimportant, for work is what most of us have to do most of the time, and our leisure is directed toward what we want to do. In one way or another, labor and leisure include the major concerns of all of us. The opening chapters of Genesis depict work and rest as conditions in which human beings to some extent imitate God himself.

It is not too easy to say precisely what work is. Different kinds of work have their own definitions, their own rules, and their own ways of admitting or excluding workers. Occupations fence themselves in for a variety of useful and practical reasons. They also fence themselves in because of a very profound human need to mark off and distinguish the things we think are important.

Much the same can be said of the non-working portion of our waking life. Again we find many special activities carried out by the members of special groups. Sports are a conspicuous and interesting example of the use of leisure. Here we find a strong tendency for leisure activity to be fenced off, in special areas, where only participants and their supporters are admitted. Some sports are carried out by professionals who are paid to play, while reporters and television people are paid to watch them! Typically, however, sports are fortunately still the activity of those who desire and choose to participate in them. For many of us, the very essence of a sport is its voluntary, non-commercial, non-utilitarian character. What trout fisherman would wish to be employed to kill fish in a fish farm, or what duck shooter would want to work in a slaughterhouse killing poultry? Although sports may be voluntary, however, they are not free and easy. Special skills, special words, special equipment, and often special clothes are all part of it. What fun would it be to go out on the gym floor, or out into the playfield, or out in a sailboat, with someone dressed in a business suit? Consider the game of chess. The human players, it is true, simply sit in chairs wearing ordinary clothes. The chessmen, on the other hand, inhabit a board of rectangles, wear exotic antique uniforms, and follow the most intricate rules of conduct. Here we see a supreme instance of the tendency of certain leisure activities to shut themselves off from the ordinary workaday world.

Of course there are many other ways in which we use our leisure. We spend private leisure time alone, or traveling, or with our families or friends. We spend public leisure in entertainments, civic and political activities, enjoyment of the fine arts, and so forth. It may come as a surprise to some of us to reflect on the fact that we go to church and participate in church activities, for the most part, in our free time.

As Christians we are of course obligated to give some of our time, both in public and private, to prayer, worship, acquiring a knowledge of our faith, and supporting the activities of the Christian community. Yet the decision actually to do so rests with us. There may be certain social pressures encouraging church going in some areas, but in North America today no adult is forced to attend church regularly. This has certain practical consequences to which we might be giving more attention than we usually do. A church will only be full because people believe it is "right, and a good and joyful thing" to be there.

This reflection brings us full circle again to the basic biblical view of work as something required in human life, and leisure—the observance of the Sabbath—as something commanded to those who recognize God as their creator.

In work we learn about things, how to use things, how to do this in order to accomplish that. We learn of the order and the interconnection of all things. To see this is to see part of what creation means. The Jewish and Christian faith is not simply the affirmation that God made things. It is rather that an infinitely wise and loving God made things good, that he made us in his image, and in spite of our sins he loves us. In the *workability* of the world, the practicality and usefulness of things, we see part of their goodness. Our own ability to understand, use and shape things is part of our kinship to our Creator.

Yet these are only half-truths. The wisdom of God is not just ingenuity; his goodness is not just practicality; nor is his love simply an adequate kindliness. The qualities of God are, as the theologians say, *transcendent*. That is to say, they go beyond, they overflow, they exceed all our categories. We cannot define his attributes; we can only cry out

O Lord our Governor,
    how exalted is your Name in all the world!
What is man that you should be mindful of him?
    the son of man that you should seek him out?

(Psalm 8:1, 5)

Or we can speak "of the plan of the mystery hidden for ages in God who created all things" (Ephesians 3:9), or sing with the angels and saints,

Splendour and honor and kingly power
    are yours by right, O Lord our God.

For you created everything that is,
> and by your will they were created and have their
> being.

(Revelation 4:11)

For this we need leisure as well as work. An executive may calculate the cost of a building, but after hours she can gaze at a sunset beyond all cost. A workman can put a beam into place, but in his garden he may watch a spider cross a chasm on a silken thread. On the job we serve by the clock, but on holiday we can observe the rhythm of waves on water, or wind in the trees, or the coming and going of children at play.

It is part of our created nature that we need the practical, useful, and reasonable things with which and for which we work. Yet it is by reflection, by considering the wonder and beauty of things without regard for their working usefulness or profitability to us, that we gain some sense of the transcendence of the God who is the source of all things.

Evolution and Fundamentalism

Throughout the lifetime of most of us, a running debate has continued between the upholders of Darwinian evolution and fundamentalist Christians who hold out for creation in seven days. For those who believe that science, and science alone, has the answer to all human problems, the spectacle is no doubt pleasing. To fundamentalist Christians, who interpret the Bible with a one-to-one literalism which the Bible itself does not follow, the combat is exhilarating. On the other hand, for those of us committed to the Anglican and Catholic understanding of creation, the evolution debates and "monkey trials" can only be depressing. It is no less depressing because it occurs in the southern Bible belt which is, in so many other ways, a particularly creative and spiritually vital part of the American scene. This broad area nurtured Billy Graham and John Hines, Massey Shepherd and the Society for the Preservation of the 1928 Prayer Book, William Porcher DuBose and the snake handlers, country music and much of the finest 20th century American literature.

One does not really know which side of this unhappy debate to feel most pity for. At one extreme are fundamentalists who see religion and life only through their own tunnel-vision spectacles. At the other extreme there is that minority of science teachers who, not having seen God at the end of their microscope or telescope, conclude God does not exist. Most science teachers, we know, are more sophisticated than that. On the other hand, in some communities the village atheist is a teacher, and most educational institutions (including the church-affiliated ones) seem to have one or more faculty members who think it is a sign of intellectual depth to poke fun at revealed religion. Needless to say, fundamentalists are their favorite prey. By fulfilling every stereotype of obscurantism, the fundamentalist is the easy target of lampoon and caricature.

Hard core fundamentalists affirm that God created all forms of life just as they are, without any evolution taking place anywhere. This is an extraordinary claim since during human history, as we know, new breeds both of animals and plants have developed, and—more regrettably—many older species have been exterminated. Faced with the fossil evidence of more primitive organisms, the most extreme fundamentalists claim that these bones and shells were created as fossils and planted by the Creator in the earth in order to challenge and test human faith!

But where do we stand? Our Anglican tradition affirms the value of scientific inquiry which has in fact enlarged and deepened our appreciation of the order and beauty of the natural world. At the same time, we affirm that this world is indeed the creation of God, who has disclosed many aspects of himself in his handiwork. It is, moreover, only as we obey his laws that we can rightly live in the world where he has placed us. Gratitude to him, and appreciation and understanding of his works, are part of the way of life to which he calls us.

The sciences analyze and describe the physical world of which we are a part, and changes and movements within it which have occurred, which do occur, and which may be anticipated in the future. The meaning, value, and purpose of the universe is not the subject matter of science, although we would emphasize that many scientists themselves are acutely aware of transcendent values. Science would not exist if scientists were not intensely committed to the belief that the natural world is worth studying.

By the same token, the subject matter of theology is not the physical analysis of the world or the living things in it, yet it is basic to Christian theology that a physical world does in fact exist. The opening chapters of Genesis do not tell us of the physical methodology by which God made the universe, but they assure us that he did.

Genesis does not tell us how long it took the world to develop to its present point. Genesis does present it in terms of a seven day week because *each week* we enter anew into the reality of God's creation. It is also presented in terms of morning (twilight, shapes of land and trees, waking of birds, etc.) because *each day* we re-experience our createdness. It is also presented in terms of spring (longer days, drying fields, growing plants, etc.) because *each year* and especially at Easter, we renew our understanding of creation. Unfortunately, fundamentalism does not usually penetrate to these levels of the mystery.

Does all this mean, as many worthy Americans have said and do say, that religion and science are totally separate routes, having nothing in common? For us, this is the worst of both worlds. The philosophic framework within which modern science came into existence depended on the coherent view of a consistent universe developed within the theism of Christianity (and, to some extent, of Judaism and Islam). Animism, Buddhism, or militant atheism, simply could not, and did not, produce it (although their followers have contributed certain items to it).

Similarly, the wonder, respect, and sense of concern which the thoughtful Christian feels toward the natural world are immeasurably enhanced by what the sciences have taught and are teaching us. Merely pious people, unaided by technical knowledge, could not treat malaria or smallpox, nor would they have alerted us to the impending lethal contamination of our water, soil, and air, nor to the near extermination of virtually all of the largest non-domesticated mammals and birds in the world today.

The understanding of physical data in science, and the understanding of meaning, value, and purpose in theology, involve different methods of thinking, but they are not concerned with two separate and disconnected worlds. Heaven help us if they ever completely part company! To bring them into a constructive harmony is the major intellectual challenge to the human race in our time.

Eagles, Skunks, and Tapirs

The problem in talking about human beings is precisely that there always is a problem. As to other living creatures on this planet, the details of their lives may happen to be largely unknown to us, but they can be observed and studied. The life of the bald eagle, or the common skunk, or the Malay tapir is lived as it is lived, and the facts are there to be discovered. But which facts, which thousand facts, will give the real picture of human beings?

An undisturbed wild eagle simply is what it is. We regard the bald eagle as peculiarly noble, but that is a human interpretation. An erect bearing, stern eye, and hook nose may connote aristocracy to us—that is, to those who have the outlook of our culture. By all means let us enjoy looking at bald eagles. To other species of eagles, on the other hand, the bald eagle's striking white head presumably looks odd. To the smaller creatures on which the bald eagle preys, no doubt its appearance is horrid. Of course, when we study the habits of our national bird, we are less approving. They eat dead things which they find, and they take fish away from ospreys that have caught them. We describe them as scavengers, and as thieves or robbers,—terms heavily loaded with emotional overtures. Yet the eagle is simply gathering food in the way that instinct directs, and dutifully takes the food home to its eaglets with no more sense of moral turpitude than an American parent purchasing a package of frankfurters at the local grocery.

To us, the skunk is a deplorable beast. Yet it simply uses its odoriferous powers to defend itself, and does far less damage to the environment than man does. The tapir with its wiggly snout is an object of humor to zoo-goers, but the animal itself gives no evidence of a sense of humor.

An eagle is an eagle, a skunk is a skunk, and a tapir is a tapir, but when are humans really human? When is a man truly manly and woman truly womanly? Most of the time we obviously are not. We must admit that in our entire lives we are not fully so. When you discuss people, you always have to be using adverbs like "fully" or "inadequately," "more" or "less," "really" or "not really," "better" or "worse."

When we speak of a wild animal as good (or bad) we mean its meat does (or does not) taste good to us, or that its fur is (or is not) valuable to us, or that it does not (or does) take food from our garden. It has nothing to do with moral virtue or vice on the animal's part. With humans, on the other hand, everything seems to have some sort of connection with virtue or vice. What men or women do is usually to a greater or less extent morally good or bad. When we talk about one another, such moral judgments are largely what we discuss. It is precisely these moral qualities that are important in human life. The "best" eagles, or skunks, or tapirs might be those of exceptional size, or of unusual longevity, or with especially handsome feathers, fur, or hides. The best men and women, on the other hand, are those of superior moral discernment, those who perceive what ought to be done, and who have the courage and perseverance to do it.

Human life is blemished and eroded by the gap between what ought to be and what usually is. The effort to close that gap, to make *what is* become what *should be* is the peculiarly human challenge; this is the distinctive calling of

people. Prophets, moral philosophers, preachers, and teachers have the uniquely human task, the preeminently manly
and womanly task, of helping us to see the gap and motivat-
ing us to endeavor to close it. A saint is not only a "better"
man or woman than you or I, but also more of a man or
woman, a more complete human being, one who is closer to
the center of the human enterprise.

Many religions (as well as nations) have used the eagle as
an emblem. Our Judeo-Christian tradition also uses the
eagle as a symbol of the transcendent. The swiftness, power,
and far-seeing eye of the eagle may teach us something
about God. The saints, however, may teach us much more.
At the simplest level, the biblical story of creation asserts
some sort of visual resemblance between God and man. The
saints take it beyond the simplest level, to that moral dimen-
sion which is the stuff of authentic human life.

The New Creation

Our Lord's baptism is a comparatively unfamiliar topic to many Christians, yet it provides extensive food for meditation and reflection. It is most prominently placed in St. Mark's Gospel, where it is the very first event he records in the life of Jesus. It is recounted in the third chapters of both Matthew and Luke, where it is the first episode in our Lord's adult life. John tells it, as usual, in his own way in his first chapter, speaking only of the descent of the Spirit on Jesus.

Mark's account is the simplest but perhaps the most striking. After briefly describing the revolutionary message and bizarre appearance of John the Baptist, he goes on,

And it happened in those days Jesus came from Nazareth of Galilee and was baptized by John in the Jordan. And immediately coming up out of the water, he saw the heavens opened and the Spirit descending on him like a dove; and a voice came from heaven, "Thou art my beloved Son; in thee I am well pleased." (1:9-11)

To begin a book with water and with the Spirit of God hovering over it like a dove, is of course to evoke powerful associations for a reader of the Old Testament. The second verse of Genesis speaks of the Spirit of God moving through the darkness over the primaeval waters. This is a fascinating and suggestive way of depicting the creative powers of the

Deity beginning to work on the inchoate and unshaped chaos.

Some primitive peoples have thought of the world as being shaped by the flapping of the wings of a legendary bird, or of the world being hatched by such a bird from a huge egg. Genesis does not describe creation in such terms, but it does evoke the memories of primitive consciousness as it suggests the archaic strangeness of the time before time. Spirit in ancient languages is also the same word as wind or breath. God's breath, related of course to his utterance or word, begins to shape the universe. God's Spirit is as the dawn wind of the new world.

When, in the arrangement of Genesis as we now have it, the world is only six chapters old, God regrets that he has made man and he plans for a flood to wash the slate clean so that a new start can be made. After the earth is inundated, it is a wind which presages the subsiding of the waters (Genesis 8:1). And here the Hebrew narrators do allow the great raven of ancient folk-lore to fan away the waters (verse 7). Finally, as we all know, it is the dove that brings to Noah the olive bough signaling the end of the flood. The entire flood story tells of a kind of second creation, a reconstitution of human and animal life on the basis of God's purpose and in conformity with his laws. The first creation depicts life in terms of emergence, efflorescence, and birth from the earth. The flood story depicts life as man and beast have for the most part known it: in terms of survival— a survival in which we see the hand of God.

For many modern Christians, to compare baptism with the primaeval waters of creation, or with the flood, seems far-fetched fantasy. For us, baptism has too often involved only a slight splash of moisture on a baby's forehead. In earlier and more vigorous ages of Christianity, larger quantities of water were taken for granted—enough water for the candidates, usually adults, to be dipped into it, which is what the Greek word baptism means. In the First Letter of Peter, there is the quite explicit comparison of baptism and the flood:

> When the long suffering of God waited in the days
> of Noah while the ark was a preparing, wherein few,
> that is eight souls, were saved through water; which
> also after a true likeness now saves you: baptism. . .
> (3:20-21)

As baptized people we are ourselves survivors of the flood, members of God's revised, purified, and restored creation. For us, this new creation does not simply rest on the basis of quaint ancient stories, but on the basis of what was really done by our redeemer, Jesus Christ. The sacrament of holy baptism unites us to him, not simply in theory or in principle, but in a real event in his life and in our lives.

2. Pruning the Apple Tree

O ye winds of God, bless ye the Lord;
    O ye fire and heat, bless ye the Lord;
O ye winter and summer, bless ye the Lord;
    praise him and magnify him for ever.

Deep Cold

The sign above the bank, on the main street of the village, flashed the time, 7:08, and then flashed the temperature at 110 degrees. We had just driven through the snow-covered countryside to the place where I catch the bus to go to work in the morning. In the intense cold, no pedestrians were visible anywhere, and few cars were moving. When it is 25 degrees below zero, and the sun is not yet up, those who are fortunate enough to be able to remain in bed are obviously doing so.

The sign above the bank entrance was now blinking 7:09. It would be four minutes till the bus was due. The temperature now showed 105; almost immediately the digits changed to 104. After the time blinked on for a second, the temperature now showed 103, changing quickly to 102. Alternating with the time, the reading descended rapidly. The bus did not arrive on time, and soon the temperature reading indicated zero.

How much farther down would it go? Whoops! It jumped up to 119 and then once more began its step by step descent. Evidently the true temperature was so cold that the electric thermometer could not handle it. Each time it labored its way down to zero, it was destined to jump back up to 119, no doubt the highest reading it was capable of—a temperature presumably never reached in Wisconsin.

For machines, as well as people, deep cold has strange consequences. Life simply cannot go on as usual. In mild

winter weather, we can generally pursue our plans and do
as we please. A warm house, heavy clothes, and transporta-
tion by automobile make it possible to follow one's usual
schedule. When the temperature goes far below zero, however, nature reaches up into our life and says, "No." We are
suddenly and sternly reminded that we humans are not
supreme. Those who ignore the warning may soon find
themselves in serious trouble.

We are instructed by the media that it is dangerous to
engage in prolonged physical exertion out of doors, dangerous to drive long distances without a blanket in the car,
dangerous to leave dogs out overnight, and so forth. Into
our normally secure and well-protected American life,
danger suddenly thrusts itself.

How do birds and animals survive? Many don't, and the
others remain out of sight. Out on the snow on a frozen
lake the day before yesterday, I saw no tracks of animals—
only a dark colored lump in the snow which proved to be a
frozen pigeon. Its wings were partly extended, as if it had
plummeted from the sky, suddenly frozen to death in mid-
flight.

Life is lived in a narrow zone, between heat that would
scorch us all to death, and cold that would freeze us all.
God has made incredible concentrations of heat in the
universe—think of the sun, only a small star! Similarly he
has created vast interstellar expanses of unthinkable cold.

Life, at least as we know it, exists only in between, in
narrow bands of moderation. Perhaps that is a cosmological
basis for Anglicanism! In any event, the sign above the bank
struggles on unsuccessfully, until at last the bus comes.

On the Ice

Winter in Wisconsin is too cold for most people, but occasionally it has its rewards. Such a reward occurred some years ago on a New Year's weekend when some of the small lakes froze over rather quickly with a sheet of clear, smooth ice. Not all lakes froze, for the deeper ones are slower, and those with a long east-west exposure were too disturbed by the prevailing westerly winds. It was certain lakes, where conditions were right, which froze perfectly. For once, snow did not follow, ruining the surface for skating.

A little ice is a common sight in the north. Ice which is covered with snow, broken and jammed ice, "white ice" formed partly of half thawed and refrozen snow—there is usually enough of that. But crystal clear, smooth, glass-like ice, stretching out like a mirror for what may be half a mile or more, that is a gorgeous sight.

One does not need to be an expert skater to enjoy getting out onto such ice. The slow plodding of pedestrian locomotion is replaced by uncanny speed as one moves freely in any direction. Leaving the shore behind, one is soon in a world of ice below and sky above. All the thoughts and concerns of ordinary life are forgotten on this new element.

Clear ice, unmarred by bubbles and refrozen snow, is often called black ice. But the clearest new ice is so clear that one simply sees the "inside" of a lake beneath. There are pale sand, clumps of green weeds, and a fish swimming here and there. One sees a foreign world of life moving

gracefully but silently beneath one's feet. Deeper water is
greenish and darker as the bottom descends mysteriously
out of sight.

Part of the fascination of being on ice is that it is different from ordinary experiences. The surface of water is
normally always moving, whether it be with little ripples or
large waves. To be out in a boat or swimming is to experience constant motion. In contrast, ice presents us with rigid
stillness, and offers the smoothest large surface to be seen in
nature. To walk, jog, or skate upon it is to taste the normally
forbidden pleasure of walking on water.

As with many pleasures, there is an element of danger
and fear. The less experienced skater fears falling. With new
ice that is not very thick, perhaps we all have an underlying
fear of falling through—which could have serious or even
fatal consequences. Although a lake has been explored and
tested by others, at the beginning of the season it takes a
certain act of faith to venture for the first time out on the
middle, over the deep water. This can be suddenly very
scary where new clear ice is "perfect" and virtually invisible
to the eye.

The snapping hiss of a crack opening up nearby can be
very frightening. Even more impressive is the yelping or
whooping of a deep crack, which may extend for a quarter
of a mile. Such cracking is a natural process as the ice
expands. Sometimes it can be as loud as thunder and quite
startling.

So the great speed and freedom of skating, and the unusual privilege of walking on water, are also combined with
fear and an awareness of our peril. Such is human life.
Our high points and our low points are closely linked. And
if a sort of faith, an undefined confidence in the beneficence
of the world, is necessary for such a small thing as skating on

a pond or lake, how much more do we need, in the perilous journey of life, a defined and directed faith in the world's Maker!

Pruning the Apple Tree

On the rare occasion of a holiday or Saturday afternoon in winter that is not too cold or too windy, I love to prune an apple tree or two. It is one of the few agricultural activities one can carry out in winter in Wisconsin, for the ground is frozen and snow-covered, and growing things are all either hidden or dormant.

Pruning is not to be entered into lightly. You can't just prune a tree because you feel like it, in the way you could cut grass, or split kindling, or shovel snow off the steps. To be properly pruned, a tree must be looked at carefully, thoughtfully, critically, even philosophically! What *should* that tree be? Should it spread more to the east or the west? Is it destined to be relatively tall or short? Thickly or sparsely branched?

One needs to walk around the tree, make a small preliminary cutting of a branch or two, and then think about major surgery. Are there one or more substantial limbs which represent a wrong direction of growth? When these are sawed off, what will the tree look like then? So one proceeds to smaller branches and the clipping of small shoots and twigs.

One is seeking to develop a relatively short tree, with well-spread, uncrowded limbs, the energies of which are funneled up into fruit, not lumber. Too high a tree is hard to pick, and high growth cuts off sunshine from the lower parts. Branches spreading too far involve excess wood, and from the weight of fruit they often break. By successive years of pruning, I like to develop a parasol-shaped tree, its foliage and developing fruit spread out to the sun, and easy to pick when ripe.

There are many fine points and subtleties to pruning. Of two branches growing too close together, which is to be pruned and which retained? Which is more likely to bear fruit this year, or next year? Which represents better lines of growth for the long-term architecture of the tree? The art of decision-making has here a field day.

After three quarters of an hour, the earth around the tree is littered with branches and sticks of every size. The limbs which have been cut off seem almost as many as those which remain. The resulting tree looks emaciated, skeletal, ravaged. Tar paint is then applied to its pale and gaping wounds.

The tree is now ready for that time, many weeks hence, when the ground will thaw, and the sap will mysteriously rise. The newer boughs, where the bark is not too thick, will blush a discreet pink, as if red blood were flowing in the veins. Soon leaves will unfold and the glory of blossoms will follow. Relieved of its excess branches, unburdened with limbs too high or too wide, the tree can then gather all its vital juices into the production of a bountiful crop of fruit.

Our Lord spoke of pruning grapevines, not apple trees, but the process is similar. By its wounds, the plant is made fruitful; by its losses it is made productive; by its curtailment it achieves its purpose. Similarly, by maintaining the discipline of pruning every year, the farmer or gardener gets his crop. By working on these cold days, he has trees well prepared for spring. By pruning thoughtfully, he develops trees which will bear well in many future years. So it is, in some little way, that one enters the mystery of life and death; one's eyes see and one's hands handle the stuff of our earthly existence.

One does not need an orchard to prune. Two or three trees, or even one, can be time-consuming. How can one complete the job when there is so much to meditate on? Really, one can't. As you drive by a commercial orchard, look at the trees. Out of fifty trees, not one has been pruned with the care and reflection it deserves! This is work for would-be theologians, or poets, or monks, not for careless day laborers!

So with our saw and shears we approach our tree, that unavoidable and inescapable reminder of our first fall in the garden, and of our redemption on that hill outside a city wall.

Old Man River

What a place rivers have played in the history of the human spirit! The Tigris and the Euphrates, the Nile, the Ganges, the Yang-tze, the Danube, the Rhine, the Thames, the Amazon, the Congo, the Mississippi, and many others! One cannot mention the great rivers of the world without a tremor, without some thrill, without some sense of the mighty drama of life on this planet.

It is embarrassing, in such august company, to mention the Ashippun, the tiny river near which I live. It has no place in the roster of the mighty rivers of the world, for the Ashippun is only a creek, the beginning, middle, and end of which are all comprised within four rural counties of Wisconsin. Yet a river, just because it is a river, shares certain characteristics of other rivers. All begin somewhere as a tiny stream and gradually gather force. All pass through a variety of twists and curves, mile after mile, past this or that feature of the countryside. All finally vent themselves at their mouths into some larger body. So they forever flow onward and onward, never returning again to their source.

"Old Man River, he just keeps rolling along."

Nothing presents more vividly to our eyes the reality of time. Ever flowing on, day after day, year after year, century after century, the river is the outward and visible sign of the inexorable flow of events, irreversible, irresistible, unstoppable. The little river, no less than the great one, goes on relentlessly. It flows on after men and women have come and gone: it flows past as we stand still upon its banks. It is both more permanent and more transient than we are. A floating stick, a leaf, a child's paper boat dropped from the little bridge, how quickly they are swept by! How many more sticks and leaves and toys have been and will be carried by these waters!

An element in the creation story at the beginning of the Bible that is often ignored concerns the sources of four great rivers—the Pishon of Havilah, the Gihon of Ethiopia, the Tigris of Assyria, and the Euphrates of Babylonia [Genesis 2:10-14]. The geography seems a bit bizarre to us. (The Bible atlas I keep at my desk is not sporting enough even to try to locate the Pishon or Havilah.) Yet the message is clear: as human beings, animals, and plants originated in Eden, even so, in the logic of the narrative, should the great rivers originate there.

This account of the beginning of all beginnings cannot ignore the beginning of rivers, any more than it could ignore the beginning of the week, of the day, of the year, or of the human life span. All were created by God in the first place. All continue to exist as expressions of his love and his wisdom. So the river, large or small, relentlessly asks us where we came from, where we are going to, and whether we are prepared to get there.

Cow Parsnips and the Tree of Life

Plants, lots of plants, go with rivers. The muddy banks of
rivers commonly nurture a profusion of growth. Along the
Ashippun, the things which grow up every year provide a
remarkable exhibition of "plant power." Leaving aside
trees and bushes, the annual growth is surprising. By the end
of the winter, the winds, snow, floods, and floating ice have
broken down and carried away the stalks and stems of the
previous year. The banks are largely bare. With the beginning of spring, however, a profusion of green shoots appear in
the soggy ground and they race upward to get the sunlight.

This seems to be highly competitive, for the tallest and
thinnest plants clearly predominate. This includes numerous
kinds of grasses, with slightly different stalks and blades,
which ultimately have differing tassles and clusters of seeds
at the top. By June, some of these are five feet high, and
they are truly beautiful as they sway in the wind. Shorter, but
still tall and narrow, are the flags and stems of the deep
blue wild iris—certainly one of the stars of the riverside.
Like garden iris, several successive flowers bloom on one stem
so that they continue to blossom for perhaps two weeks.

The oddest plant is the cow parsnip, of which I see many
from our house. Rapidly putting up a hollow purple stalk,
it is six feet high or more in a few weeks. Clusters of leaves
jut out at intervals of about a foot. Near the top, this slender
giant sticks out angular branches that terminate in flowers
which are a curious product of plant geometry. Each of
these has a center from which two dozen or so little stems

stick out in all directions, forming a sphere the size of a baseball. From the tip of each little stem, a further little sphere of smaller stems is formed each ending in a little nib which, I suppose, is the actual flower.

Gardeners will recognize the similarity to parsley, celery, or dill plants going to seed—all the same family, of course. These globular compound blossoms are greenish, whitish, or purplish in successive stages, and are found in different hues on the same towering and somewhat grotesque plant.

A patch of wild plants differs from cultivated ones most conspicuously because of the random variety. We normally plant a field with just one crop. Vegetable gardens have a variety, but each is normally segregated into its own row. It is in a flower garden that we more commonly imitate nature by having a mixture of species. In a flower garden we also usually seek profusion, the concentration of many plants in one small area.

In the classic garden plan, there is a fountain or pond in the middle. There is something deeply satisfying about the cluster of blooming growth around a small body of water. Beyond the beauty of individual flowers, the whole arrangement gives expression to vitality, to the emergence and fertility of life. This is quietly refreshing and restoring to the human spirit. Along a green river bank, we see something of the same thing in uncultivated form.

For the Bible, a transcendent river bank is the final description of heaven. "Then he showed me the river of the water of life, bright as crystal, flowing from the throne of God and of the Lamb through the middle of the street of the city; also, on either side of the river, the tree of life with its twelve kinds of fruit, yielding its fruit each month; and the leaves of the tree were for the healing of the nations" (Revelation 22:1-2).

Animals Seen and Unseen

As a river has its plants, so too it has its animals. Some are creatures directly linked to the water, and others are there because of the shelter provided by riverside vegetation. The Ashippun, the little river I see from my house, has quite an assortment.

Let us not begin by discussing mosquitoes! They are all over Wisconsin, by the millions. It is more pleasant to start with the damselfly, the gentle cousin of the dragon fly with dark iridescent wings and long, thin, black body, which flits along by the water's edge, stopping here and there to perch on a bent blade of tall grass or on a bulrush. This is but one of the many very pretty insects along the stream.

There are fish in the water, of course, at which local anglers occasionally try their hand. There are frogs, and no doubt salamanders, in the marshy places. Twice this spring a turtle has come up onto our lawn. Once, a medium-sized snapper, settled on our road soon after 6:30 in the morning when I was going off to work. To avoid hitting it with the car, I got out, grabbed it by the tail, and flung it aside while it snapped at me ferociously.

The name of this sort of turtle is well deserved. Unlike most turtles, they have relatively small shells, but big strong legs and long tails slightly suggestive of an alligator. Their large, ugly head can dart out as quick as a snake and bite in any direction, while, their baneful eyes glare at you most ominously. Their horny white jaws look like they could

clip off a person's finger or thumb in an instant, although
in all honesty I have never heard of anyone being bit by one.
Killed and cut up, they are the basis of several different sorts
of delicious soup. No doubt there are plenty of snakes along
the river, too, but I have yet to find one.

What about mammals? The "Wind in the Willows"
world of small animals is again largely unseen. There are
muskrats and mink here, and upstream there are aspens
felled by beavers—but only once has anyone in our family
seen one. Other animals, such as deer and rabbits, we have
seen in the adjoining fields, but in the thick vegetation along
the river they are always well hidden.

Perhaps best of all are the birds. Some Canada geese nest
somewhere nearby and often fly low overhead. So too do a
pair of mallards. We sometimes see a great blue heron and
also a little blue. On rare occasions, a kingfisher is perching
on a dead limb or a telephone wire. And of course there are
droves of red-winged blackbirds. All of these are in addition
to smaller and less conspicuous denizens of trees, bushes, and
high grass along the banks.

It is ironic that there is so much to see, but this is only
the smallest fraction of the animated life that exists along
this stream. One does not expect to see all the worms,
insects, and water creatures, but one would like to see the
noisy tree toads that sing in the spring, or the babies of the
wild geese, or the parade of mammals that drink from the
river or forage along its shore every night. This must range
from tiny shrews and mice, on up to coons, foxes, and deer.
What is seen is almost inconsequential compared to what is
unseen!

We think of the spectacle of nature, the tapestry of
nature, the almost kaleidoscopic changing picture of nature—
but most of it is no spectacle at all, for we cannot see it.
Most wild animals live most of their lives invisible to us. In

these terms, we all grope through life like blind people, unable to see most of what is going on around us. Nor do we hear it, feel it, or smell it. The natural world, as it exists at our very doorsteps, infinitely exceeds what we perceive.

This is not a new thought. Ben Sirach, the author of the Book of Ecclesiasticus in the Apocrypha of our Bible, expressed this very well over 2,000 years ago. After enumerating many wonders of God's creation, he concludes, "When you exalt him, put forth all your strength, and do not grow weary, for you cannot praise him enough. . . Many things greater than these lie hidden, for we have seen but few of his works" (Ecclesiasticus 43:30, 32).

As the Sand on the Seashore

For many of us, nothing is more characteristic of summer than a trip to the beach. To lie on the beach is, for many, the ultimate in relaxation, idleness, and separation from the cares and hubbub of life. Yet even in idleness our minds keep moving. Indeed, we sometimes find that it is in idleness that our minds have a chance to move.

We do one kind of thinking when we work—usually rigid and canalized thinking along certain specified lines. The thinking we do when lying on warm sand, on the other hand, knows no channel. It can wander in any direction, consider any memories or hopes, compare ideas, feelings, emotions, and associate things with the shapes of clouds, or the movements of the water or the configurations of the sand before our eyes.

We can relax on a beach because a beach, the very sand itself, is outside the normal boundaries of life, outside the ordinary rules of how things are supposed to be. Sand can be washed by waves, blown by wind, and trodden by human feet into endless patterns and configurations. At the seashore, where the tide is ever active, beaches change every day. Inland, they usually change more slowly, yet it takes but one good storm to move a great deal of sand.

Sand can be poured, pushed, kicked, piled up, or scattered about. With care we can shape it and mold it. Yet it always resists the straight lines, the vertical surfaces, and the rectangular shapes with which we surround ourselves in our work-a-day world.

Of course, sand is used in concrete, mortar, and building blocks, but in its natural state, on the beach, sand is a stubborn opponent of the rectilinear and mechanical organization of human civilization. It summons us to a different kind of space, to a realm of curved, irregular, undulating, and transient forms.

People relate to beaches differently. Some insist on folding chairs, carefully spread towels, and rubber shoes to keep the sand out of their toes. They may even take the *Wall Street Journal* to the beach to read! The clothes one wears, or does not wear, are also part of it.

People who wear ordinary clothes are not likely to sit on the sand. People who come in warm sweaters to walk briskly along the shore in early spring or in the fall certainly enjoy it, but they too do not sit in the sand. It is when our clothing is reduced to bathing suits, or when we take everything off our small children, that we are prepared to get down on the sand, to crawl on hands and knees, to be warmed by the sun, and to be splattered by the wet fur of dogs.

In the ordinary course of daily life, we have opportunities to hum or whistle tunes. We can doodle or draw pictures on bits of paper if we feel so inclined. We can even make up a line or two of verse. Yet most of us have no opportunity at all to model things, to mold, to form shapes.

At the beach, freed from our ordinary clothes and our ordinary inhibitions, we can dig little ditches, pools, and tunnels. We build hills, pyramids, or castles. If ambitious, we can even form recumbent statues—although they rarely come out quite as we expect. Here we have the tactical experience of shaping things with our hands which is so basic to human reality, yet so infrequent in our mechanically ordered modern world.

The *Venite*, psalm 95, says, "The sea is his, for he made it, and his hands have molded the dry land."

The word "molded" is striking. I am informed that the late W.H. Auden, the renowned poet, chose this word for the translation. It is a felicitous choice, expressing vividly the creative work of shaping by hand. At the beach we see the water God has made, and we can experience for ourselves something of molding. Not only the biblical image, but the biblical feel can regain for us its force.

Yet our molding is obviously very different from God's. The Psalms speak of his works which are permanent—at least to the extent of lasting millions of years. Our works are very transient, and this is never more vivid than at the beach. No castles are so shortlived as sand castles.

Perhaps this is a melancholy reflection, yet it is also part of the fun! Who would want to go to a beach where all the castles never washed away? Or who would want to dig all sorts of little holes and tunnels in his front lawn where they would have to be endured all summer? On the sand we enjoy our little constructions which only last a day, and at the same time learn humility about our serious projects which often last longer than they deserve.

Haymaking at Sunset

What an evening there was yesterday! Instead of the silver
sunset so common in Wisconsin, the western sky blazed with
gold as the sun descended to the distant horizon. Far to the
southeast, large rounded pink clouds rose into the sky,
flattening off at their tops into wide pale sheets. In the east,
the great white disk of the full moon swung up into sight,
before the setting sun was entirely gone.

I had a grandstand view, standing on a haywagon with
some parishioners as we hurried to get a load of hay in
before the predicted rain in the night. We faced first one
side of the glorious sky and then another, as the lumbering
old tractor made its way round and round the field. It drew
the bailer which picked up the hay from the ground and with
strong thumps pushed it into bales, tied each with two
strands of twine, and pushed the bales, one by one, up a long
shoot toward the wagon being towed along behind, where we
grabbed them and placed them symmetrically, like big bricks,
on the wagon.

Such an evening does not often occur, and of course it
always passes too quickly. It must be enjoyed for what it is,
gratefully and without regrets. Few things express so clearly
the transient quality of life as a gorgeous sunset. It is the
most beautiful part of the day, but it also signals the day's
end.

For Holy Scripture, hay is the great symbol of the short-
ness of life, for today the plants of the field are green and
growing, but they can be reduced to hay by the bright sun of

a single hot day. While using several different words for
grass, hay, and fodder, the Old Testament speaks of this
again and again.

Evildoers "shall soon wither like the grass" (Psalm 37:2).
"In the morning it is green and flourishes; in the evening it
is dried up and withered" (Psalm 90:6). "I wither like the
grass" (Psalm 102:11). Such expressions occur repeatedly.
One of the most notable of these passages is in Isaiah 40:6-8.
"All flesh is grass, and all its beauty is like the flower of the
field . . . but the word of our God will stand forever."

For us today, hay is also a notable symbol of the difference between agriculturally based rural life and commer-
cially based urban life. Nothing is more common in the
country than hay. It is in fields and in barns, and bits of it
are in your car, your hair, and your boots. Yet nothing is
rarer in town. There simply is no use for it in the modern
city, except occasionally to feed the animals when a circus
comes, or to feed the two or three cows and sheep which
are incongruously exhibited at the zoo.

So the evening and the hay come and go. The big buildings of the metropolis also have their rise and fall, "but the
word of our God will stand forever."

Cold Water

Some weeks ago, when summer had just begun, southern
Wisconsin went from being quite chilly to being thoroughly
hot. Although I had not noticed other people in swimming,
I felt the water in the small inland lake near which I live, and
I concluded that the time had come to begin the season. I
had had a long and tiring day at the office, and a swim would
do me good.

Yet I seemed to have a certain reluctance. I attended to
several chores first, until the descending sun in the western
sky warned me that I had better begin. My family were all
away, and I would have to go to the lake alone. The waters
were a beautiful rippling blue.

Of course, I realized that the water would feel colder to
my feet than it had to my hands, but when I stepped in,
somehow it was even colder still. The bottom at that point
consists of small stones—two kinds in fact. Some are round,
smooth, and slippery. Others are sharp and hurt your feet.
So I stumbled and lurched forward into the icy waters. As
I went further, the water level was like a searing ring of iron
slowly moving up on my legs. It was too late to retreat.
Shivering, I pressed on painfully as the water got deeper.

I, like many others, have never enjoyed wading into cold
water. It helps to think of the fact that many other people
have endured much worse pain—martyrs have been sawed in
two, and so forth—but it doesn't help enough. After years of
such wading, by the time I got to be about 50, I accepted the
assurances of those who say it is better just to dive in and

have it over with. They are correct, and now, in my years of wisdom, I usually do dive straight in, without even feeling the water. But such bravery is more than I can summon on the very first day of the season.

Now, half-way in and having endured enough pain, I plunge forward. The coldness of the water is lost in the splash and the sudden effort to begin swimming. In a moment it feels wonderful. Cool, yes, but very refreshing. After swimming around a little, I get out, catch my breath, and jump in again.

How odd it is that one goes through a few minutes of excruciating suffering in order to enter the water. It hurts more than cutting your finger with a knife, or burning your hand on the stove, or having a bad bump or bruise. It is physically more painful than anything else I normally experience in a day. Yet cold water does no harm at all. Once one is all the way in, the water suddenly feels good, so good that people travel long distances to reach beaches, build expensive pools, and vie for waterfront properties.

This experience of painful entry into the water seems to be a paradigm of many other experiences. We use many figures of speech derived from it: "try the waters," "wade in," "take the plunge," "immerse oneself." Such phrases are used in business, politics, education, and social life.

Such phrases are peculiarly applicable to Christianity. The waters of Holy Baptism are the distinctive sign of becoming a Christian. If we grew up outside the Christian sphere, and only heard the Gospel as adults, we would indeed hesitate to enter the font. If, as in the Roman Empire or in some Islamic or communist countries today, being baptized meant risking one's life, the first steps might indeed be agonizing. Where adults are baptized, as is preferable, by going right into the water, what a shock it must be, followed by relief that the step has been taken.

Most of us have not experienced our religion as a decisive and resolute plunge. After a lifetime, most of us are still hesitantly stumbling forward on slippery rocks, only a little way from shore. May the Lord in his mercy help us at last to dive forward and swim!

Field of Corn

Yesterday afternoon I threaded my way through a cornfield. Most of the corn was far over my head. The stalks rose straight up, in bamboo-like rows of glistening green. At every joint, the leaves stretched out in deep green arch-like curves in row after row after row.

I was cutting across the grain, as it were, going at right angles to the rows in which the corn was planted. I had to choose my steps carefully, here a little to the left, where there was an extra gap between stalks, and there a little to the right where, perhaps, a smaller stalk allowed more space to pass through.

The corn was obviously luxuriating in the hot weather, growing an inch or two each day and each night. Within the field it created a whole green world of its own, a world invaded by wild sunflower plants (also sending up tall sturdy stalks), but not many other intruders.

In a few weeks, the ears will form and ripen, and in due course the stalks will die and turn tannish yellow and the stiff dead leaves will rattle in the wind. So it will follow the biblical pattern, of life, death, and life, a parable of the Resurrection.

Of course, when our Bibles speak of "corn," they are referring to wheat, in accordance with British usage. Our American corn, or Indian maize, was not known or referred to in the ancient literature either of the Hebrews or the Greeks. Nor did the biblical writers speak of rice. Yet these three great food crops, wheat, American corn, and rice are all related (all are obviously members of the grass family, along with oats, rye, bamboo, sugarcane, milo, and numerous other plants), and together they make up the basic dietary network on which we depend. All die as they yield their grain for the next season.

There it is, the stuff of earthly life, in its shiny green inscrutable mystery. Some grow well, some are stunted, some die prematurely. Yet many plants yield many dozens of kernels. There is that parable of the sower (Mark 4:13-20). If you don't understand this, how do you expect to understand the harder ones?

The sheer vitality of God's gifts is amazing. Seeds want to grow. They will push through rubbish, leaves, small stones, and other obstacles to do so. "What's the opposite of gravity?" a fellow in the country once asked me. "Anti-gravity," he declared, answering his own question, "and plants have it!" Indeed they do. Pushing up, extending leaves, flowering, and bearing fruit are what plants expect and desire to do, and they will overcome surprising difficulties to do so. At the same time, these plants all will die and bequeath their vitality to a future generation.

This is what we eat, unconsciously perhaps and unknowingly, as we eat bread. Not simply the force of life, but also the inevitability of death, and the promise of a life beyond. Wheat, corn, and rice will not do all of that alone, but they point to the One who can.

Many ancient people worshiped a corn god. We do not need to be embarrassed that in some sense we do, too. "I am the living Bread which came down from heaven . . . the Bread which I shall give for the life of the world is my flesh" (John 6:51). The Holy Eucharist is the completely appropriate expression of the Lord, who promises that his disciples "will come from east and west, and from north and south, and sit at table in the kingdom of God" (Luke 13:29).

Down in the Briar Patch

Picking blackberries in a briar patch on a late summer's day is a most relaxing and carefree activity. There are no disruptive telephone calls, no urgent messages arriving at one's desk, no unanswered letters, no unwashed dishes, no unpaid bills, no unmade beds, nor other irritating tokens of the never-completed tasks of modern life.

In the briar patch, all one has to worry about are pricks and scratches from the briars on one's hands, wrists, ankles, and face, tears in one's clothes, irremovable berry stains on one's shirt, stings from wasps and hornets that are working the same vines, harassment from neighbors who accuse one of trespassing, and, in some parts of the country, snakebites.

Why is it, one wonders, that berry vines, which seek to attract birds, humans, and other creatures to eat their berries and so to scatter their seeds—why, oh why, do they at the same time seek to repel us and punish us with their multitude of sharp little thorns? Or if, conversely, they are really trying to drive us away and remain undisturbed, then why have they spent millions of years evolving such sweet and delicious fruit?

One answer is quite simply that the good things in life are only bought at a price. Because freshly picked wild blackberries are so good, expect a few drops of your blood to be shed! Experience tells us that there is a good deal of truth in this. Beautiful flowers are hard to grow, talented children are hard to rear, beautiful ladies are proverbially hard to woo, and handsome husbands are said to be hard to live with. Quality, excellence, and virtue are rarely achieved easily.

As a philosophical principle, this may be profound, but it still does not tell us why blackberry thorns are so sharp. After all, the plant has no awareness of philosophical principles, and, if it did, this would hardly help vines to grow, their flowers to bloom, or their seeds to be disseminated.

Inexplicably, the items on the grocery counter of life continue to have their price tags, and the ultimate legal tender is not dollars, but blood. For blackberries this is truly ridiculous, for real red blood is literally shed—yet the quantity is so small as to be irrelevant. We remember it only, if at all, when we later see the reddish-purple juice of the fruit.

For some more serious things, such as war or childbirth, much more blood is literally shed. For most things nowadays, the blood is more theoretical, or at least less visible to the public. A man who struggles with a difficult and demanding job today may have a bypass operation. Three hundred years ago, his ancestor instead may have lost an arm in a sword fight. Blood remains thicker than water, and the red blood we share with all other warm-blooded creatures is a solemn reminder that we are all part of a mysterious cycle of life and death. The red juices of certain fruits point to the reality of an even wider kinship.

In today's world, we have largely lost the sense of the spiritual significance of the cycle of life and death. At the purely physical level, the varied life of this planet, embodied as it is in millions of species of animals and plants, will, according to present projections, have been largely exterminated within the next hundred years.

Rain forests, the world's reservoirs of oxygen, are being chopped down as fast as American and Japanese-made chain

saws and bulldozers can cut them. Commercial hunters
relentlessly pursue the few remaining sperm whales and wild
elephants. Smaller and less dramatic species, containing
unique chemicals, and performing unique functions in nature,
are being exterminated each year. Not only are lakes and
rivers polluted, but yellow rain is poisoned even before it
falls from the sky, and wells will soon be bubbling with water
already contaminated in the underground aquifers.

A race which cannot appreciate the physical amenities of
the earth on which we live is not too likely to appreciate
transcendent spiritual values either. The final cost is paid in
blood—blood well shed or wrongly shed? Blood for the life
of the world, or against the life of the world?

The red juice of the crushed berry, the thorn drawing
blood on the hand or brow, the wasp sting ("O death, where
is thy sting?"), the torn and stained shirt (fleeting memories
of Isaiah 63!), the serpent at the heel are all small reminders
of the realities underlying the mystery of our existence.
There are many chalices, large and small, on the altar of the
world. All point somehow to the covenant; all may put us in
remembrance of things which we would too gladly forget.

Autumn Mist

The sun shines with a bright white light. Between the clouds the sky is a cold blue. The clear air permits one to see far, far into the distance. The vegetation is no longer an undifferentiated sea of green; instead, the landscape is now divided into discrete sections.

Here is a brown, newly ploughed field. Next to it is a hayfield still gorgeously green. Beyond is a stand of corn, now yellowish tan. A bushy strip is marked by scarlet sumac leaves. Further off, a grove of larger trees is turning yellow and orange. Yet in another direction the winding line of willows along a creek is still bright green. In the summer it had all blended together. Now, in the fall, the countryside is sorted out into precise and logical parts, each clearly visible in the bright light. Rationality seems to prevail.

Then comes the mist. Reaching out with fumbling fingers, huddled in oddly shaped clumps and clusters, or spilling out in broad flat sheets, the mist gently swallows up details of the landscape, swaths fall colors in a greyish white, and blurs our vision. Its beauty is of a different kind. It is fascinating and strangely interesting.

It is as if some other order of reality, some earlier stage of creation, has quietly crept up to the surface to reassert its claims on the earth we see and know. In defiance of the rational landscape of autumn which we see so clearly, the mist silently reminds us of the mystery of what we do not see or understand and cannot grasp with our hands.

It rises over ponds and lakes, creeks and rivers, and the

swampy ends of fields. No doubt its appearance is entirely explainable in physical terms involving air, moisture, and temperature. Yet this explanation is totally invisible to our eyes. Usually mist appears on clear, cool mornings, but this is not necessarily so.

Over the creek near our house, it sometimes rose up on a summer evening, making a small wraith-like column between the trees, like smoke from a small bonfire. A mile upstream, where the same creek winds through a shallow valley, the mist spilled out, these same evenings, in a film of gauze over the top of the adjacent cornfield.

The world involves what we see and what we don't see, what we understand and what we don't understand. What is only partially perceived, like mist, may have special meaning and beauty for us. This is as true of human relations as it is of the external things of the landscape. Mystery, no less than clarity, is part of what God has made, and is that with which the universe is adorned.

3. Summer Nights

O ye days and nights, bless ye the Lord;
   O ye light and darkness, bless ye the Lord;
O ye lightnings and clouds, bless ye the Lord;
   praise him and magnify him for ever.

Moon Time

There is nothing that speaks more consistently or more dramatically about the mystery of our existence than does the moon. In earlier ages it was feared too much exposure to moonlight would make one insane—*i.e.*, a lunatic. Today, when even in rural barnyards overhead electric lights overwhelm our view of the night sky, a willingness to take time to look at the moon becomes a rare sign of sanity.

All of the moon's successive phases have their distinctive charms, but the full moon is in a class by itself. Its circularity gives a unique sense of plentitude, balance, and perfection. Although we have seen the face of the moon countless times, we can always gladly look at it again. We first see a new moon just after sunset, a sliver of white in the western sky. We encounter the quarter or half moon well up in the sky at nightfall. The full moon, on the other hand, rises just as the sun sets, and it may do so in many guises.

A so-called paper moon seems to be a fragile, thin, and semi-transparent disk, raised on the blue surface of the evening sky. Or, seen through damp atmosphere in the eastern sky, the full moon can rise lemon yellow, or in the riper yellow of a yellow apple. Or it can be a delicate peach color, or the bold pumpkin color associated with autumn.

The moon looks incredibly big as it rises over trees, houses, hills, or fields in the east. It gradually seems to pull itself from the earth and finally soar up, bit by bit, into the sky.

The emotional effect of seeing moonlight on land or on
water is matched by our awareness of its other influences.
We know it draws the tides of the ocean. It seems to affect
the behavior of various living things, including the human
reproductive cycle. It may, as many have claimed, affect
our minds and feelings in some way. It is not surprising
that primitive peoples have performed religious ceremonies
by its light. Sunshine affirms the here and now of ordinary
workaday existence. Moonlight affirms that there are other
dimensions of reality.

For the Christian church, the full moon has a unique
role in marking the central event of our calendar. Easter is
(in principle at least) the first Sunday after the first full
moon after the spring equinox. As more and more of us discover the fullness of the Easter celebration in the Great
Vigil of Saturday night or early Sunday morning, we come
face to face once more with the full moon which was the
original marker of the paschal feast.

The year that we enter the church just as the full moon is
rising, or go to church or return from church by its light,
makes an indelible impression. Here is creation's own witness
to redemption. Here nature points to nature's Lord. Here the
inanimate creation itself celebrates the glory of the resurrection.

For those who have had this close encounter with the
paschal moon, full moons at whatever season can never again
be a mere circle of secular light in a secular sky. Spring,
summer, fall, or winter—every month they remind us that our
spiritual ancestors crossed the desert and the Red Sea, and
that on just such a night the Lord rose triumphant from the
grave. This is infinitely more important than so much of
what we think about, talk about, or worry about. It is worth
at least a few minutes of our time one evening a month.

Sabbath Time

Space stretches out in all directions, while time seems to flow
relentlessly one way. To measure space we pace it off, or use
measuring rods, tapes, chains, surveying instruments, or
odometers. Time, on the other hand, always seems to emerge
in measured units. Like bamboo poles, it is marked off at
fairly regular intervals. Nature offers us many units which
the inhabitants of this planet *may* use to measure time. It
offers two units which *must* be used: the day and the year.

The ever on-going sequence of days and nights is the most
conspicuous phenomenon that consistently occurs on the
face of the earth. Sub-terranean fungi and creatures living in
the depths of the sea may ignore the sun. The comparatively
few creatures which live in the arctic or antarctic circles have
the odd experience of six months of light during the summer
and six months of darkness during the winter. Yet most of
the higher animals and plants necessarily base their own
daily life cycle on the alternation of light and darkness.
Human beings may get up and go to bed earlier or later than
the sun, but by and large our life is shaped and arranged in
24 hour cycles. We could not do all our work on Monday,
all our eating Tuesday, all our drinking Wednesday, all our
talking with other people on Thursday, and all our sleeping
on Friday. Our life is a daily life; we generally require all of
these activities each day. A well ordered day is the basis of
sane and wholesome life. Nature has left us little choice.

The same is true with regard to the year. The annual
cycle of summer and winter, seed time and harvest, or (in

the tropics) rainy season and dry season, is of overwhelming
importance to most plants and most animals, including
ourselves. We cannot disregard it.

Yet while day and night and summer and winter are
forced upon us, there are many other intervals of time that
nature measures off which are not so drastic, and which we
may or may not allow to govern us. Days may be subdivided
down into hours, minutes, and seconds, or added up into
weeks or other groupings. Then there are months originally
marked by the moon, and the seasons marked off by the
equinoxes and solstices. The seasons are of course important,
but their exact divisions are not so clear to the naked eye.
Income taxes in our civil life and Ember Days in the church
are more or less intended to precede these quarterly divisions,
but have both undergone some dislocation.

How important all of this has been for human culture!
Without divisions of time we could never plan works involving many people. Agriculture, construction, travel, com-
merce, and government all deal with measurable time. Without our ability to measure time, to add or subtract divisions
of it, even the crudest civilization would be impossible.

Religion is sometimes thought to be timeless, but for the
faiths looking to the God of Abraham, namely Christianity,
Judaism, and Islam, religious observances are heavily involved
in ancient and tradition-laden intervals of time. Personal
prayer, according to our monotheistic heritage, should be
offered to God by believers every day. Prayers for guidance
in the morning, the Lord's Prayer with its petition regarding
daily bread, and prayers for protection in the night, all pre-
suppose daily recitation. We also have great observances and
special occasions which recur every year. In between the
daily and the yearly cycle, Christians, Jews, and Muslims
have public worship every seven days. Why seven? Might not
six or eight have done just as well? Or is this a quite arbitrary

decree of the Hebrew God, to be judged by no canon of
human reason? No doubt many believers have assumed the
latter. Yet God's decrees are rarely whimsical.

Many biblical references associate the Sabbath with the
new moon, as in II Chronicles 2:4 and 8:13, Isaiah 1:13, and
Ezekiel 45:17. We presume that originally the seven-day
week was simply a four-fold division of the 28 day lunar
month, reflecting the four quarters of the moon. In fact,
however, the lunar month is not exactly 28 days, and after
the sequence of weeks had become rigidly standardized, the
weeks gradually got out of step with the months.

For primitive peoples the moon is of course the calendar.
For people living much of their life out of doors, with little
artificial light, the phases of the moon are very evident.
For those planning to hunt, travel across the desert, sail in a
ship, or make war by night, the presence or absence of the
moon can be very important—even for modern peoples. For
seafaring folk, the lunar cycle of the tide is crucial. For
women there is the physiological cycle of their own bodies.
Many farmers, probably all over the world, base certain
agricultural practices on the lunar month.

Unlike the sun, the moon appeals more to our emotions
than to our reason. The sun forces us to wake in the morning,
makes us perspire in our work, and leaves us exhausted when
it retires at night. The moon, on the other hand, does not
bludgeon us, but rather gently summons us on those evenings
when it appears. It spreads a glittering veil on the landscape,
and paves a silver avenue across the water. Its mighty tidal
power over the sea, and its still inexplicable connection with
the daughters of Eve—all this sets the moon in a realm of
mystery. The elegant horns of the new moon, the growing
face of the half moon, and the glorious round disc of the full
moon are all evidence that God did not make the universe on
purely pragmatic or materialistic lines.

Genesis says the heavenly bodies are all to "be for signs and for seasons and for days and for years" (1:14). The Son of Sirach says that God

made the moon also, to serve in its season
to mark the times and to be an everlasting sign.
From the moon comes the sign for feast days,
and a light that wanes when it has reached the full.
The month is named for the moon, increasing marvel-
ously in its phases, an instrument of the hosts on
high shining forth in the firmament of heaven.

(Ecclesiasticus 43:6-8)

The Sun Coming Forth

The first article of the Christian faith, our belief in God as the maker and creator of all things, affects our view of anything and everything. It is not easy to picture God existing by himself from all eternity, beginning to make everything out of nothing. Nor is it easy to picture any alternatives. To imagine that everything which now is has been from all eternity, this is also to dumbfound the mind. Neither poetic imagination, nor common sense, nor the science of physics find it congenial to speak of an ever-existing universe. Neither is it easy to join our atheist friends and suppose that everything just happened to come into existence because of an accident. It is hard to picture an accident occurring before there is anything to have it!

For our ancestors long ago, and for our spiritual forebears who wrote the Bible, it was also difficult to picture how everything came into existence at the dawn of time. For them, as for us, it was helpful to consider those entries into existence which we ourselves can see or feel. The most obvious personal experience of something like creation is the return of day every 24 hours. This is one of the most characteristic events on the surface of this planet. After the death-like non-consciousness of sleep, we awake, we find ourselves alive again, and we enter a new day. If we awake early enough, we will see the dawn. After the darkness of night, a gray twilight comes first. The dawn wind stirs. The shapes of clouds become visible. Soon we can see the face of the earth spread out, and trees, bushes, buildings, and bodies of

water appear. The sun itself emerges above the horizon in
glory. Birds are noisy, and if we live in the country, we will
hear other animals too. In due course we ourselves, the last
created, emerge onto the scene.

    Man goes forth to his work
    and to his labor until the evening.

                                        (Psalm 104:24)

Did you ever think that this, among other things, is what
the first chapter of the Book of Genesis is talking about?
The dawn of all things is suggested, subtly and with restraint,
in terms of dawn as we know it. Of course many of us nowadays *don't* really know it. We stay up late at night and
arise under duress in the morning, more interested in getting
our first cup of coffee than in seeing the sun as "it comes
forth like a bridegroom out of his chamber" (Psalm 19:5).

    For most of us a more vivid sense of renewal and the
re-experiencing of creation occurs annually, in the spring.
As the short days and cloudy wet weather of winter are
passed, the warmer bright days and the returning green of
plants and trees affect most people very deeply. Those in the
country watch the returning birds and hear the singing of the
frogs in the hollows, while city-dwellers flock to parks and
public gardens. The first chapter of Genesis is talking about
this too, poetically overlaying the dawn and the new year in
those mysterious archetypal, cosmic seven days.

    To reflect upon the Bible, to enter into the sacred his-
tory, to go through the threshold which it opens to us—to do
this requires a certain give-and-take, a thoughtful and reflective exchange between our life and experiences, and the
words of the Scriptures. As we do this, we discover that
things are indeed made new, we are made new, and we catch
a glimpse, we feel a throbbing, we hear a whisper of the
meaning of that ongoing mystery of the creative power of
God.

Summer Nights

Summer days should be pleasant; so too should summer nights. The night is indeed an important time. The Bible often speaks of the darkness as the setting within which God discloses his presence. This is a topic, as we shall see, which has become something of a problem for many Christians today.

But what does the Bible say about the night? The psalms offer interesting examples. In Psalm 8, the psalmist acclaims the glory of God and his handiwork in the heavens. The moon and the stars are cited, not the sun. Plainly it is the night sky that the poet is contemplating. Psalm 74, verses 15 and 16, now among the opening sentences for Evening Prayer, ascribes to God the day, but "also the night," and he is praised as creator of both sun and moon. In Psalm 139, the author seeks to flee in the darkness, but finds darkness is not dark to God, "darkness and light to you are both alike."

Darkness can be a time for eating and drinking, for talking and story-telling, for singing and dancing. It can also be a time for thinking, meditating, and praying. The pressure of daily work is past. Darkness covers over, at least for most people most of the time, our places of work, our tools, the multitude of things we look at and worry about when we are on the job. The workaday world of hammers and saws, of telephone dials and typewriter keys, of levers and switches and buttons—all this melts away in twilight.

Night spreads a veil over the earth, and for the hours of darkness it is a new and different world, a world of feelings,

imagination, human values, deep perceptions, and insights.
The proper illumination of the nocturnal hours—candlelight,
lanterns, firelight, lamplight, fireflies, and moonbeams—all
these disclose a very different world from that of daylight.
This world of night is one to be enjoyed, explored, and valued.

It will be noted that in the first chapter of Genesis, in the
epic of creation, the darkness precedes the light of the first
day, and each subsequent day involves first evening and then
morning. For us Gentiles, a new day begins an instant after
the stroke of midnight. For the ancient Hebrews, as for
modern Jews, the new day begins at evening, at sunset. It is
on Friday evening, at the end of the sixth day, that Jewish
families gather around the dinner table, the mother blesses
the candles, and the Sabbath begins.

Similarly, on Saturday evening the Sabbath is over. We
see this in the gospels when the crowds came to Jesus on
Saturday evening, when Sabbath rules are terminated, *e.g.*
Luke 4:40. We still observe relics of this in the liturgy, when
we begin to use the Collect for Sunday on Saturday evening,
or on important feasts which are intended to begin with the
preceding Evensong.

Why did the Hebrews think of the new cycle beginning in
the evening? Partly, no doubt, because the sky was their
calendar. It was during the night, when you saw the moon
and stars, that you could determine the date. But surely too
it was because of the distinctive character of night. It was
apparently on the holy nights that the great feasts were observed with banquet, song, and dance.

So we still find, at the midnight mass of Christmas and
Easter, that there is ultimately no conflict between night as a
time of sharing in the deepest mysteries of our faith and
night as a time of joyful song, of wearing our best clothes, of
conviviality with relatives and neighbors.

The canticle *Benedicite* in Morning Prayer calls upon the nights, no less than the days, and darkness, no less than light, to bless the Lord. Night is a time in which you and I too can bless and call upon the Lord.

The Night of Life

The Bible and our own human experience offer many
thoughts about that half of our created existence which is
shrouded in the night. Our reflections on it may be concluded with that final earthly topic—death. At night, as in
death, we lie down, we are silent, we go out of communica-
tion with the world. Sleep, as all the world knows, is a figure
of death.

Asleep, furthermore, we enter the land of dreams. Here
we, no less than our remote ancestors of bygone centuries,
find dead friends and relatives to be very active. Such en-
counters, if they are hostile, can be distressing and trauma-
tic—indeed, trauma literally means a bad dream. If frequently repeated, these experiences can be overwhelming. On the
other hand, a pleasant visit with a deceased loved one, if we
may speak respectfully, is worth a hundred visits to a psy-
chiatrist.

Sleep also resembles death in its resignation. Lying
down, we make ourselves defenseless; we close our eyes, not
really knowing when or whether we will open them again;
and we trust that the lives of others will go on without us.
Christian spiritual teachers encourage us to view going to
sleep as practice for a holy death. The clause, "Into your
hands I commend my spirit" (Psalm 31:5), is the basis of the
dying words of Jesus (Luke 23:46) and of the first martyr,
St. Stephen (Acts 7:59). These words continue in use as a
bedtime devotion of countless Christians and as a familiar
versicle in the Office of Compline.

Preparation for death is one of the typical themes of Christian devotion in the evening, and at Evensong we follow ancient words of the church when we pray "that we may depart this life in thy faith and fear, and not be condemned before the great judgment seat of Christ."

This is an aspect of night that is sober, but not necessarily sad. When the day has been passed and our prayers have been said and our loved ones have been kissed, nothing is more pleasant than to go to sleep. So too, in the peace and fellowship of the church, our earthly life can conclude with a contented death. We do not know what the waking will be like, but if we have seen the truth of God's salvation in this life, we can "depart in peace," according to his word.

The Meaning of Blackness

Both the Bible and human experience affirm the importance of night, its place in the sequence of life, and the importance of both good and bad things associated with the night. Yet this is not the whole story. Some particular parts of the Bible use light as the symbol of the power and goodness of God and, correspondingly, associate darkness with evil. In view of the dependence of earthly life on sunshine, this is a natural and not inappropriate symbolism. It is, after all, one of several symbolisms used by different biblical writers.

This particular usage is characteristic in the Old Testament of the books of Job and Ecclesiastes (*e.g.,* Job 3:5-4, 18:18, 30:26, and Ecclesiastes 2:13-14). In the New Testament it is conspicuous in the writings of St. John, as in the famous verses: "In him was life, and the life was the light of men. The light shines in darkness, and the darkness has not overcome it" (John 1:4-5). It is also strongly expressed in Ephesians 5:8-14 and elsewhere.

It is to be noted, however, that these references to light and the dark mean illumination and its absence; they do not refer to white and black as colors. The Bible often uses white in reference to clothing, and speaks of black and white as colors of horses (Zechariah 6:2-6; Revelation 6:2 and 5—but note that the most ominous horse is "pale" or yellowish, verse 8). In regard to pigment of human skin, "black" or "dark" is not often used. On the other hand, "white" is used repeatedly of human skin, namely in association with the dread disease of leprosy (see Leviticus 13).

At one point in the Bible where racial prejudice based on skin coloration may be implied in regard to the Cushite wife of Moses, the complaining sister of Moses is punished by God in being afflicted with leprosy and turned to the color of snow (Numbers 12:10)! This does not, of course, mean that racial prejudice is absent from the Bible: rather it was based on other factors, notably circumcision.

It is in modern times, on the other hand, and in modern languages, that one sees a move from light/darkness symbolism to white/black. Such phrases as blackhearted, the black side of someone's character, or the verb to blacken, seem to be part of a comparatively recent European and American culture.

In a world in which large numbers of people are described as ethnically black, it hardly seems appropriate to continue the use of the adjective black as a symbol of evil. It is not a biblical symbolism. Christians believe all people are created in the image of God. We should not use words in ways which block the understanding of such basic biblical teaching.

The Circle of Past and Future

Human life consists of constantly looking ahead, no less than looking behind. My day today cannot be just like yesterday. I can indeed get up at the same time, put on the same clothes, and so forth, but even if I try to repeat all the actions of 24 hours ago, the lives of others will interfere. Different people will telephone about different things, different mail will arrive, and so forth.

Nor will nature allow a complete repetition. The daylight is going to be a little longer today, and it seems a little warmer. The treacherous bit of ice scraped off from the front doorstep yesterday is no longer there to be scraped off today. Yet it snowed a little in the early morning hours, and now there is snow to be swept off the back steps.

I cannot again split logs for the fireplace before supper as I did yesterday evening, for that little pile of logs is now all split. Two or three dry pieces have indeed already been burned. Never again, in the entire history of the world, are those very same molecules likely to come together again in the same way in one tree!

Tomorrow, and tomorrow, and tomorrow will all be a little different, although most days will have some framework of similarity. As I grow older, I realize it is counterproductive to expect constant innovation. I cannot usefully attempt to say entirely different prayers each day, or adopt a different approach to my work, or eat meals at totally different hours. Habits are necessary. How could one

possibly remember all the things one has to do each day
without habits?

People who wish to avoid all change are simply being
unrealistic. But so too are people who welcome all change.
We cannot even function physically, much less mentally and
spiritually, if too many things change. Jet lag, as many
travelers know, is the debilitation caused by a mere change
of two or three hours more or less in a day.

It seems to me that a certain rhythm, a certain balance
of continuity with change, is what one needs for a sane and
reasonable life. Nature provides the model. Day and night
follow each other in an unbroken order, and the yearly
cycle of the seasons never fails. Yet each day is a little
different, and every so often one day is very different.

The pattern of nature has been followed in the liturgy.
Daily Morning and Evening Prayer follow the same pattern
day after day, while psalms, lessons, and other items within
that pattern vary. The Holy Eucharist generally adheres to
the same framework every Sunday, but again specific items
within the pattern vary. Occasionally, there are very special
days which break the pattern, but there are few such days in
a year. This is a good pace for human living.

Yet one cannot end the discussion there. All of us hope
for something more, either for ourselves or for those whom
we love, beyond the mere repetition of calm days, weeks, and
years. It is a real question, how much or how little to hope
for in this life. Those who hope for too much, risk grave
disappointment. Those who hope for too little will easily
be passed by.

Americans have seen so many innovations in so few
years—radios, airplanes, television, space exploration, com-
puterization—that we are ready to hope for a great deal. It is
a shock to us to learn that for untold centuries, in many parts
of the world, many people hoped for no significant changes
whatsoever.

Of course primitive peoples hoped for a good year—
a healthy baby, a good run of salmon, or a good crop of
sweet potatoes—but absolutely no one hoped for a heated
swimming pool, a tractor with an air-conditioned cab, or a
newly redecorated bathroom! Many primitive peoples, so
far as we know, hoped that the unbroken order of the life
they knew, hard as it was, would continue indefinitely.
Women did not aspire to practice gourmet cooking, but to
cook just as their great-grandmothers had done in olden
times. Men did not aspire to hunt with a new kind of bow
and arrow, but rather to be excellent marksmen with the precise kind of bow and arrow used by the great hunters of the
legends of the past.

To recapture and reembody the heroic stature of the
sacred ancestors was the ideal. By trying hard to do what
they already knew how to do, primitive peoples overcame
incredible obstacles and survived every sort of adversity.

Let no one laugh at our stone-age ancestors! Their lives
were simple and close to the earth, but what is wrong with
that? The vegetables raised in your own garden, the egg
laid by your hen, the fish you caught in the river—you too
will find them better than the richest offerings of the super-
market! To build your own house as our ancestors did, or
to nurse your own baby, or to hike up a mountain or to swim
across a river, all of these do have their unique satisfactions.

The hopes many of us have for our own future are
indeed closely linked with our perceptions of a somehow
more glorious time in the past. What has been and what will
be are somehow tied together. In at least some ways, there
is a circularity. If we can learn to live with the cycle of
nature and the annual cycle of the seasons of the church,
then we can be accepting and understanding of this paradox
in our perception of time and in our perception of ourselves.

Getting Ready

Notable portions of the church year are seasons of preparation, but this is the way life is, too. We survive, and other creatures survive, by being prepared. The bird cannot wait until all the food is gone before it migrates south; the frog cannot wait until the pond is frozen to go to the mud in the bottom; nor can the groundhog wait until December to accumulate the fat to nourish him through his long winter's sleep.

Our ancestors could not get through the winter if they waited until two feet of snow was on the ground before they started looking for firewood. Nor could we mine enough coal or pump enough oil or natural gas to get through the winter if we waited until late fall to start.

Life requires getting ready, either instinctively, as animals do, or by choice, as we do. Our choice is not always easy. We admire people who build up their savings, who get snow tires on their car long before the first snow, and who have all their Christmas cards mailed before December 10. Yet we don't admire them too much. Many people have lived and died in penury, saving for a future that never came, and what is the fun of Christmas shopping in October?

Often we have to force ourselves, or be forced by society, to make preparations of an important sort. Nature itself usually doesn't force us until it is too late. When we are forced to build a fire in very cold weather, it is too late to accumulate and dry our firewood; when we are sick, it is too

late to take regular exercise; when we are dying, it is too late
to lay careful plans for a will.

At any point, the time we experience has been prepared
for in the past; the time we experience is preparing for the
future. Mundanely stated, the toast you ate for breakfast
was made from grain milled long ago, which had been grown
long before that. The pencil I have just sharpened, to use
Milton Friedman's famous example, was manufactured from
materials gathered from all over the world. The present, like
a thick delicatessen sandwich, is made of many layers.

The good use of time is the good use of what we can
harvest from the past, and what we are planting for the
future. Stewardship of time is stewardship of life itself. As
John the Baptist preached, we must get ready.

Incarnation and Light

It is as the manifestation of the glorious light of God our
Creator that St. Paul spoke of the incarnation of our Blessed
Saviour. Some other writers of the New Testament expressed
similar thoughts. But how do the writers of the four gospels
relate the Lord's coming among us to the doctrine of creation, the first article of our Christian faith? We may
approach this by also considering their use of the symbolism
of light and the related theme of darkness as the space within
which light manifests itself.

St. Matthew, immediately after speaking of our Lord's
birth, proceeds to tell of the magi, the wise men from the
East. It is a star—certainly seen in the darkness of night—
which finally brings them to Bethlehem. This of course is
uppermost in our thoughts on Epiphany. St. Mark does not
provide any information about our Lord's birth or childhood
but, as we shall see next week, Mark has his own way of
relating the beginning of the gospel to the story of creation.
St. Luke has the most familiar account of our Lord's birth in
Bethlehem. Around this, in turn, has crystallized the popular
imagery of Jesus, Mary, and Joseph in the barn surrounded
by animals, an attractive pictorial way of suggesting the cosmological implications of the incarnation. But returning to
the theme of light, Luke develops it in connection with his
poetry. In the *Benedictus* or Song of Zechariah, the forgiveness of sins to be announced by John the Baptist is

> Because of the tender mercy of our God
> Whereby the sunrise (or dawn) from on high will
>   visit us
> To shine on those who sit in darkness and the
>   shadow of death . . .

>   (Luke 1:78-79)

This comparison of the coming of redemption to the rising
of the sun suggested long ago the use of this canticle in the
morning devotions of the church, where we continue to
recite it. The angels' song, "Glory to God in the highest,"
(Luke 2:14), is introduced in the previous verses by the
appearance of the angels and the shining of God's glory in the
night. Then there is the *Nunc dimittis* or Song of Simeon
(Luke 2:29-32), in which salvation, embodied in the child
Jesus, is called

> A light for the enlightenment of the Gentiles
> And the glory of thy people Israel.

These poems or canticles, together with the *Magnificat* or
Song of Mary also given in Luke's gospel, have of course had
a far-reaching influence on the development of Christian
worship, especially on the daily morning and evening prayers
of the church.

It is in the fourth gospel, St. John's, that this theme of
light comes back into explicit relation with the doctrine of
creation. When John wrote his gospel, he began in a solemn
manner, reminiscent of the opening of Genesis: "In the
beginning was the word. . . ." As God had begun creation by
making light, so now it is announced, "In him was light, and
the light was the life of men. . . ." There are no shepherds or
wise men in John's prologue, but in his own manner he tells
us what the incarnation means. Jesus Christ embodies the
intellectual light, the truth, the meaning, and the divine purpose on the basis of which all that exists has been consti-
tuted. It is on this same basis that our rationality as human

beings is possible ("the light of men"). But "light" suggests more than rationality. It is the faith, it is love, it is the goodness of God which illumine the heart and which make us truly human. It is this light, which is in Jesus Christ, that the Creator of the universe wills to share with you and me.

Will you see this light? It is most likely to be consciously experienced, by you and me as by shepherds and wise men, in darkness, quietness, and solitude. Tonight perhaps? Will you leave the circle of lamplight and venture out, to stand alone beneath the winter sky, experiencing darkness for a few minutes? It is in our darkness, our inner as well as outer darkness, that we can receive some vision of the light of Christ, in whom we behold the glory of God the Father.

The Watches of the Night

At every moment, half of the world is dark, and half of our lives are spent, knowingly or not, in the night. Night is a time of rest, a time (for most of us) to cease work, a time for social conviviality and for individual reflection. It also may be a time of loneliness, of discouragement, and of danger.

All of these different moods are reflected in the Bible, particularly in many familiar psalms. Regarding rest, Psalm 4 at Compline says,

> I lie down in peace; at once I fall asleep;
> for only you, Lord, make me
> dwell in safety.

Regarding conviviality, Psalm 81 summons us; it seems clear that some feasts are partly celebrated at night, when the new moon and the full moon are seen:

> Raise a song and sound the timbrel,
> the merry harp, and the lyre.
> Blow the ram's horn at the new
> moon
> and at the full moon, the day
> of our feast.

Corporate prayer at night is expressed in the familiar Psalm 134 at Compline, addressed to those who "stand by night in the house of the Lord." As to individual prayer, Psalm 63 puts it so well:

My soul is content, as with marrow
and fatness,
and my mouth praises you with joyful lips,
When I remember you upon my bed,
and meditate on you in the night watches.

As we seek progress in the spiritual life, what Psalm 63
has said bears reading over. Modern books about religion
do not usually say much about this. Yet older devotional
manuals, such as *Preces Privatae* of Lancelot Andrewes, or
Holy Living by Jeremy Taylor, regularly provide devotions
for use when we cannot get to sleep, or when we wake up in
the night.

At such times, any of us may occasionally think of our
Creator—but usually we do not. Our minds are more likely
to turn to impatience, to irritation at not being able to sleep,
or to depressing reviews of the problems and unresolved
issues of the past day. To turn consistently to God at such
times, to put him first in our thoughts, is something of an
acquired art. It involves discipline and practice.

A Prayer Book and Bible on a bedside table, and a cross
on the wall at the head of our bed, may help remind us.
Learning to pray in these vacant and often lonely spaces in
our life opens a new field of prayer. When such a time has
been well used, many will find that they fall into a peaceful
and especially refreshing sleep. On the other hand, night
really is a time of danger. As to enemies, Psalm 59 says,

They go to and fro in the evening,
they snarl like dogs and run
about the city.

Describing the natural order, Psalm 104 speaks of dangerous animals,

You make darkness that it may
be night,

in which all the beasts of the
forest prowl.
The lions roar after their prey
and seek their food from God.
The sun rises, and they slip
away
and lay themselves down in their dens.

Psalm 30 reflects authentic human experience when it says,

Weeping may spend the night,
but joy comes in the morning.

For those in sickness, sorrow, or bereavement, dawn does often bring relief, hope, and a new sense of vitality.

The daily cycle of activity and repose (whether we work by day and sleep by night, or *vice versa* like the beasts of Psalm 104) is integral to the life we know as it has developed on this planet. Both the activity and the rest are essential to our earthly existence. The inexorable round of day and night will never allow us to forget it. We can receive our days and our nights grudgingly, as involuntary slaves of the system, or we can do so freely and gratefully, as the sons and daughters of our Creator, who wait in joy for the dawn of eternity.

Eve and Mary

The events of human life are strangely complex. They do not simply happen in an instant. Any important decision, any course of affairs, any significant occurrence, has behind it earlier developments, preliminary steps, and preparatory actions. Similarly, the consequences and results, and a variety of sequels, stretch out into time afterward.

The stories at the beginning of the Bible, told as they are in rather brief and sometimes severe terms, recognize this. This is very evident in the third chapter of Genesis, in what is familiar to us as the story of the Fall. First, the serpent persuades Eve to eat the forbidden fruit and then she persuades her husband, and then after he has eaten, the consequences of disobedience are pronounced by God and their practical effects are later experienced.

The writers of the New Testament see this story being reversed. It is the good purposes of God which lead to the incarnation of our Lord and his works of redemption which bear subsequent fruit in our lives. A key passage for this line of thought is the fifth chapter of St. Paul's Epistle to the Romans. Adam, says verse 14, is "a figure of him that was to come." Why? Because Adam was the primal, archetypal figure of humanity. In biblical thinking, he represented the whole of humanity ("the whole human running race," as Corita Kent has called it) which was to be descended from him. Centuries later, it would be Jesus Christ who would become the primal, archetypal figure of humanity. Verse 19 says:

For as through the one man's disobedience the many
were made sinners, even so through the obedience of
the one shall the many be made righteous.

But prior to the disobedience of the "one man," Adam, was
the faithlessness of Eve, tempted by the serpent. Even so,
prior to "the obedience of the one" was the faithfulness of
Mary, inspired by the Holy Ghost. Although our salvation
was uniquely accomplished by Jesus Christ, it is a many-
layered event, involving many other people in many ways.
The motherhood of Mary is a part of it very much in the
Christian consciousness as we approach Christmas.

St. Paul was the first writer, so far as we know, to compare explicitly the story of creation with that of redemption. The close relation between creation and redemption
was also alluded to by other biblical writers. A century
later still, it was taken up at length by St. Irenaeus of Lyons,
whose thought has inspired many subsequent Christian
thinkers and who remains the inspiration of much charac-
teristically Anglican theology. For Irenaeus, the interpene-
tration of creation and redemption is the key to the whole
Christian outlook. It is because God really did make this
world and make us in his image, that God the Son could
enter the world in human form. We had been so formed in
the first place that the Lord might come among us, and
be one of us. Jesus, brought into the world by Mary, undid
what was done by disobedient Adam and Eve, so that the
heirs of redemption, the children of the new birth, might
experience a new creation, the renewal of all things. For
some of us, this remains one of the most exciting things
about the Gospel—the discovery that creation is made new,
and can be experienced and re-experienced in new terms.

Eve was created to be queen of the world. Like all
things human, this queenship has been blurred, tarnished,

hidden, distorted, misunderstood, misapplied, confused. In
a wonderfully unexpected way, it reemerged into light in a
humble young woman in an obscure corner of the Roman
Empire.

4. Seeing Creation

O let the earth bless the Lord;
  O ye mountains and hills, bless ye the Lord;
O all ye green things upon the earth, bless ye the Lord;
  praise him and magnify him for ever.

Seeing Creation

You and I did not see the Hebrews pass through the Red
Sea. Nor did we see the battles David won or the temple
Solomon built. Nor did we see Jesus healing on the Sabbath,
or giving out the loaves and fishes by the lakeside. But we
have seen and do see God's works of creation. Furthermore,
we see more of them than did any of the sacred writers of
the Holy Scriptures. They saw little more than the southeast
corner of the Mediterranean world, with its rather limited
repertoire of plants, animals, birds, reptiles, and fishes.
Today every school child knows about polar bears from the
North, chimpanzees and gorillas from Africa, penguins from
Antarctica, and kangaroos from Australia. We all know
something about caterpillars becoming butterflies, tadpoles
becoming frogs, and salmon swimming up rivers to the place
where they were hatched.

The stuff of creation is literally before our eyes, under
our noses, and to be heard, tasted, and touched. Of all the
great doctrines of Christianity, the evidence of creation is
everywhere that we are, all about us, and also within us, at
all times and in every circumstance. Every day of our lives
we see God's handiwork, and can constantly admire and
wonder at the ingenuity and beauty of what he has done—
even in the most common things, a blade of grass, a pebble,
an insect, a puddle of water, or a cloud overhead.

Yet here is the curious thing. Christians, or at least
many Christians, "see" this. Lots of other people don't.
These latter include many scientists who certainly know

much about the balance, order, and multiplicity of the
natural world. They include artists who see the colors and
shapes of this world with especially acute eyes. And the
non-seers include millions and millions of ordinary folk
who seem to pursue their course through life without
bothering about the wonder, beauty, or possible meaning
of the universe about them. Like the pagan idols of old,
"eyes have they, but they cannot see. They have ears, but
they cannot hear" (Psalm 135:16, 17). In short, nothing is
more evident and open than the imprint of God's hand in
the world of which we are a part, and yet it is evidently
hidden to so many, including some who are certainly
thoughtful and perceptive observers.

We will not convert poets or painters by telling them to
exaggerate the pink in a rosy sunset. We will not convert
musicians by urging them to put more notes in an already-
rich chord. Nor will we convert scientists by arguing that
evolution took a longer or a shorter period. On the contrary, we can only encourage them to recognize and articulate the wonder of what they already know, and to acknowl-
edge to themselves and others the even greater wonder of
what is yet to be mastered. Great artists or scientists are
usually humble in the face of their own subject matter.

Ultimately, it must be the Holy Spirit who opens our
eyes in a new way, who shows us the universe in a new light.
It is the Spirit who must initiate life by brooding over the
waters. Once we have recognized the universe as the work
of God, it is difficult to see how it could be viewed other-
wise. Here, as so often in other ways, grace enables us to
do what, perhaps, an unfallen human race should have done
naturally. When we come to know that our true home is in
a heavenly country, we for the first time can appreciate this
world properly.

Yes and No

The way to God, as spiritual teachers of many faiths have declared, is a way of *yes* and of *no*. We learn of him both through what is, and through what is not. God declares himself in the rising sun each morning, and we receive from him the new life of a new day. Yet all the things we see and hear and do during the day fall far short of God. We find God in another way when darkness falls, when we cannot see or hear or do so many things, when life becomes quiet, and we feel the vastness of the night. Precisely in this withdrawal from the innumerable sights and sounds and activities of the day, we can turn to him who is also above and beyond all of his creatures, the Eternal One who cannot be seen by mortal eyes or touched by our fingers of clay.

As with the day so too with the year. The vitality, pleasure, and romance of spring give us each year a new vision of the reality of creation. The blue sky, the green grass, the colors of flowers, and the songs of birds all betoken the loving power and wisdom of God. Yet the God of heaven and earth is infinitely more than can be disclosed by a field of flowers, or a returning flock of red-winged blackbirds. As we learn of God by the resurgence of natural life each spring, so we learn of God also by the withdrawal of such life each fall. God is also present in the bare bough, the cold sky, and the brown and wilted stalks and leaves along the roadside.

All flesh is grass,
    and all its beauty is like the flower of the field.
The grass withers, the flower fades,

when the breath of the Lord blows upon it;
surely the people is grass.
The grass withers, the flower fades;
but the word of our God will stand forever.

Isaiah 40:6-8

Both in the coming and the going of natural life, both in
its affirmation and its denial, both in its *yes* and its *no*, we
learn of the God who is above all times and seasons, the One
who is eternal, holy, and true. So to the Christian there
is meaning in the fact that sunset is as beautiful as sunrise,
and the fall is as beautiful as spring. The scarlet vein in an
autumn leaf is a poignant reminder that its sap is akin to
our blood. Leaves also return to earth as we do, and plants
drop seeds which (like many of our good deeds) will not
bear fruit until another season.

In the biblical book of Ecclesiastes, there is a poem
expressing similar thoughts which was widely sung as a
popular song some years ago.

For everything there is a season,
and a time for every matter under heaven:
a time to be born, and a time to die;
a time to plant, and a time to pluck up what is
planted;
a time to kill and a time to heal;
a time to break down and a time to build up;
a time to weep, and a time to laugh;
a time to mourn, and a time to dance. . . .

Ecclesiastes 3:1-4.

For Christians as for Jews it has always been important to
observe the seven day week with its recurring times of public
worship. Catholic Christianity is also deeply sensitive to the
dailiness and yearliness of our lives. This is, in part, what the
church's daily services of Morning and Evening Prayer are

intended to express. It is part of the way also that the individual Christian learns to perceive the place of the thread of his or her life within the vast tapestry of which we are a part.

The Fireplace in Lent

In early spring there are still evenings when an open fire is welcome—indeed there are many such evenings in Wisconsin. Its warmth, its cheerfulness, what can only be called its companionship, are still welcome.

An open fire is an extraordinary example of the power of a symbol. Very few American homes which are equipped with fireplaces, Franklin stoves, or open gas ranges actually are dependent on these open flames for essential heat. Yet a cheerful bright flame can convey more to the heart than a steam radiator does to the body.

For perhaps a hundred thousand years, a fire has meant to human beings warmth, security, and companionship. Its symbolic power is so great that it can make us feel warm, even if we are chilly, make us feel safe, even if we are not, and the fire itself can offer us congenial company in the absence of human companions.

What does a fire say to us with its crackles and murmurs, its dancing flames and glowing embers? Its message is what it is: it is not translatable into human words. Many of us would agree, however, that it says more than the endlessly droning television set at the end of the room, which has become the backdrop to so much indoor American life.

Fires, having been the focal point of human social and family living for so many millenia, connote and express life. Their sound and movements are animated and vital. Like living organisms, they move, they breathe oxygen, and they need food. In a fireplace, like a domestic animal in a pen, they patiently wait for us to feed them. In the wild, as in a dry forest or on a prairie, they ravenously seek their own food, they grow, and with their sparks they disseminate offspring.

Yet fires put before us the riddle of life and death. In an hour, a fine oak log is reduced to crumbling charcoal. An hour later, we see nothing but a shovelful of white ashes. Sturdy wood which took so many summers to grow, so much sunlight, so many rains, is here reduced to only a fine powder. With shocking speed, the drama of "earth to earth, ashes to ashes, dust to dust" has been enacted. These ashes can soon go out on the vegetable garden, and start the cycle again in another form.

We can also burn what we wish to destroy—old leaves, old papers, old clothes—things we wish to forget, as well as to get rid of. Both sociable warmth and powerful destruction provide the symbolism of the lamplighting prayer for Lent: "Almighty and most merciful God, kindle within us the fire of love, that by its cleansing flames we may be purged of all our sins. . ." (BCP, p. 111).

The Bible associates fire with the presence of God, with the Holy Spirit, and much else. At this season, we may recall its association with sacrifice. Fire, which can destroy so much so quickly, expresses the removal of things from this earth. Fire, which replays so rapidly the cycle of life and death, expresses both vitality and mortality. Fire, with its endlessly changing shapes and colors, defies human categories: the dance of the flames points to transcendence.

In ancient times the connection of fire with sacrifice was also pragmatic. Part at least of the sacrificed animal was usually eaten: the fire cooked it. In the Old Testament, sacrifices are regularly offered by fire, and sometimes they are accepted through miraculous flames (Judges 6:21 and 13:20; I Kings 18:38).

Fire still speaks to us of conviviality and pleasure, and

also of sacrifice, destruction, and the mysterious cycle of life and death. Burning candles on the altar mean more than pleasant decorations. The Epistle to the Hebrews, 10:5-10, citing Psalm 40:7-9, proclaims that burnt offerings are abolished by Christ, who offered himself, in obedience to God's will, as a perfect sacrifice for the whole world. Yet even in explaining this, the Epistle to the Hebrews must allude to burnt offerings in order to explain what our Lord's sacrifice means.

As long as chilly weather lasts, we will be content to look at the cheerful flame, knowing that it also has solemn lessons for us. Ultimate companionship and friendship, the reality of human community, will be found in the circle of that mysterious and invisible flame which illuminates the cross of Christ. In his accepted sacrifice is our salvation, our reconciliation, and our peace.

Gardener's Prime Time

Gardening is among the very best of human activities, and in most parts of our country, June is the best of times for gardeners. Flowers, fruits, berries, and vegetables are coming in, and there is the promise of much more on the way. Here we see, feel, smell, and taste the bounty of the earth and the results of our own labors.

Gardening may involve an oversized plot, with fruit trees, vines, bushes, and rows of different sorts of flowers and vegetable produce, the maintenance of which is or should be a full-time job. Or it may be a solitary plant in a pot beside the bed of an invalid or disabled person. In either case, it will bring unique satisfaction to those who tend growing things.

Age is no barrier. Young children can learn a great deal from assuming responsibility for a few plants, and the old can be consummate gardeners. I remember my wife's grandmother, well on in her nineties, moving deftly through the rows of her garden. Though nearly blind, she could spot ripe berries or ripe beans faster than a young person. In winter, she gently patted and greeted the plants growing indoors, and seemed to be able to make anything flourish.

A garden is a sort of world in miniature. Here, in a small space, order can be established, and its results can be seen. We make plans, we plant, and in a few weeks we begin to reap results. Of course we must wait. Agriculture is a perpetual exercise of surrendering present ease in order to gain future satisfaction. But the satisfaction does almost surely

come, and once the process is begun, things grow with
surprising rapidity, as our Lord reminded us in the Gospel.
This does not mean that a garden is a miniature Eden.
There is digging to be done, and there are too many slugs,
weeds, and dry days. Yet when this work is done, the
results show, and at least some Eden-like qualities may
appear.

Human beings are so created that they need to do useful
things, and they need to understand what they are doing.
Unlike animals, we cannot simply repeat endless programmed
actions without seeing the results. Unfortunately, in today's
world, many of us are employed to do work which leads to
no direct results which we can see or benefit by. We fill out
endless pieces of paper which, perhaps, ultimately facilitate
the manufacture of some obscure product we ourselves do
not use or would not use even if we had the opportunity.
Customers we never see buy it for purposes we will never
understand. For countless modern men and women there is
an alienation between themselves and their work. Loss of
interest, discouragement, and frustration result.

To enter one's garden is like leaving the "modern world"
and entering the "real world." Here we plant seeds and set
bulbs which, if we care for them properly, do grow. Our
vines yield green beans, which we can pick and enjoy at the
dinner table an hour later. Our peonies bloom and bring
beauty, fragrance, and joy to the same table. Here a mean-
ingful relation is reestablished between thought, work, and
beneficial results. These results are concrete and material,
and at the same time communicate something to the mind
and spirit.

The opening of the Bible appropriately places mankind
in a garden. In the last chapter of Revelation, the scene is
a kind of magic orchard. By the grace of God, some of that
good magic is there to be had on these June days—"the leaves
are for the healing of the nations."

Gardening is good for the mind and body, offering moderate but regular exercise throughout a good part of the year. It also has great spiritual value. One of the unique things about gardening is the direct reward of one's effort. If you do the right things at the right time, or at least *most* of the right things *almost* at the right time, you generally get the desired results some weeks or months later. These results are not in doubt, they are things that can be directly enjoyed by your eye, your nose, or your palate, and they can bring similar pleasure to your family and friends.

Yet this is only the beginning of the matter. The gardener does indeed plan and work. Yet the gardener does not create seeds, or rain, or sunlight. We only cooperate with a vast network of forces much greater than ourselves.

If a gardener develops a new strain of seed, as he may, or artificially irrigates, or even artificially illuminates, it is only by delving deeper into the forces of nature and cooperating with them in different ways. Finally, it is up to the seed to germinate and grow. We can only watch, with wonder and delight, as those tiny seeds give birth to new plants, which resolutely push up their stems, unfold their leaves, and carry out the extraordinary processes of photosynthesis whereby they make living stuff.

The gardener must work, as the ant more or less explained to the grasshopper, yet in the garden, human work is always reduced to scale. It is always part of a larger whole. The gardener must plan, yet the fragile wonder of one leaf or petal of a plant far exceeds all that the gardener could plan.

In the garden we see both the important role of human care and responsibility, but we also see its limits, its relatively small place in the larger whole. In the garden we can actively and consciously be part of that larger whole. Here is the sense of the transcendent which many gardeners feel, as they stoop in the hot sun, or struggle to pull recalcitrant weeds, or dig manure or compost into their plot of soil. Here the wonder of the universe is discovered, not by reading books, but by seeing, smelling, touching, and tasting.

The one perfectly tuned, perfectly tempered, perfectly adjusted human being, our blessed Lord, was very much at home with living things, and spoke of them constantly, seeing expressions of God's power and handiwork everywhere. We ourselves, at least on a small scale, can improve our relation to God's universe by going out and getting our hands in the soil.

Saint's Day on Saturday

The Saint's Day fell on a Saturday, a beautiful clear Saturday in early June. I entered the country church where I was visiting, chose a pew on the left side near the front, and knelt as did the several other worshipers. Soon the priest came in, we stood, and the liturgy began, "Blessed be God, Father, Son, and Holy Spirit. . . ."

We sat as a member of the congregation went to the lectern for the first two readings. My eyes strayed out the open window to my left. Across the parking lot were green bushes and high grass. Beyond that was a hayfield, ending with a slight ridge, along which was an irregular row of trees, their leaves glittering green in the sunshine and light breeze. Beyond the trees was the pale clear blue of the sky on a summer morning. The reader's voice recaptured me: "Set apart for me Barnabas and Saul for the work to which I have called them."

After the Holy Gospel, we sat again, and the priest read a passage about St. Barnabas. The chirping of an unidentified bird again caused me to gaze out the window, across the cool green countryside, to the distant trees standing against the sky, holding up their glittering leaves toward heaven. Is that what the saints are like?

The priest's voice soon brought me back. "At Lystra in Asia Minor, the superstitious people took them to be gods, supposing the eloquent Paul to be Mercury, the messenger of the gods, and Barnabas to be Jupiter, the chief of the gods, a

testimony to the commanding presence of Barnabas . . ."
(*Lesser Feasts and Fasts,* p. 244).

I remembered the passage from somewhere in Acts.
Paul said, as best I remembered it, "Turn instead to the God
who made heaven and earth . . . he did not leave himself
without witness, but sent rains and fruitful seasons." The
God of the hayfield is indeed the God the holy apostles
preached.

At the peace, smiles and nods were exchanged all around.
I leaned across the pew behind me to reach to two friends
back of me. In a semi-rural county like this, many of the
members from the different small Episcopal congregations
are at least slightly acquainted with one another.

There was no server, and as no one else offered to do so, I
went up to bring the bread box and cruets to the priest at the
offertory. "The Lord be with you. . . . Lift up your hearts."
The priest proceeded, "We give thanks to you, O God, for the
goodness and love which you have made known to us in
creation." The trees in the distance were no longer irreverent
intrusions. And a little later, "presenting to you, from your
creation, this bread and this wine."

Here it was: all fields, all bushes, all vines, all trees, all
somehow are gathered, brought forward, and offered up
beneath the cross. "In the fullness of time, put all things
in subjection under your Christ." Let all be well, and let all
manner of things be well. Even so come, Lord Jesus.

Communion, closing prayer, and dismissal followed.
Then silence. No need to listen further to any human voices.
No need to look out or to look in, to look up or to look
down. In silence the world could momentarily stop. Then,
recreated, life could once more begin.

Barefoot on the Path of Life

In August, it is permissible for adults in the United States
to go barefoot, at least at some times and in some places.
It is not usually permitted in places where people are working (unless one works as a lifeguard or something like that)—
which seems a way of admitting that barefootedness is a
privilege and a pleasure, not to be mixed with the unpleasant-
ness of work that one is paid to perform.

I knew an old gentleman who was deeply shocked, on
entering a small nonscheduled commercial airplane, to
discover that the pilot flew without shoes. Many of us would
no doubt feel the same if we entered the office of our
lawyer, doctor, or dentist and found him or her barefooted—
although I have heard that Abraham Lincoln took off his
shoes in his presidential office in summer.

Be all that as it may, there is something special about
those times (rare times for most of us) when we can walk
across grass, or smooth stones, or a smooth dusty path, and
feel with our toes and soles what we are walking on. Perhaps
we can even let ourselves go and, like small children, walk
barefooted through a puddle or stream, and enjoy the splash
of the water and the soft stickiness of the mud.

Barefootedness gives us a vivid sense of where we are, a
perception of presence. We are no longer insulated and
armored against our environment; through our feet it presses
into us and becomes part of our consciousness. When your
skin is against the earth, you are really there.

113

People of many faiths walk barefoot when on a pilgrimage, and the reason may be deeper than ascetic self-discipline.
The two possible occasions in the Episcopal Church for
which one might perhaps have one's shoes removed, baptism
by immersion and the footwashing on Maundy Thursday, are
exceptional, but highly impressive.

I have always had a secret sympathy with those Oriental
religions which require one to take off one's shoes before
entering their holy places. I have been impressed by the
reverence of Anglican priests from India who remove their
shoes before celebrating the liturgy. If you are seriously
coming into the Lord's presence, then it makes sense to do as
Moses was commanded to do, and remove your shoes
(Exodus 3:5).

On the one occasion I was in India, some twenty-five
years ago, I was taken to visit a Hindu temple in Mysore.
Passing the beggars and cripples huddled at the entrance, I
took off my sneakers at the doorway, like my guides. I
reluctantly sank my stocking-clad feet into what I imagined
was the slimy filth of the floor. Inside, I soon forgot my
inhibitions. There was plenty of incense. A chanting priest
was handing out blessed flower blossoms to worshipers.
Seeing my white cassock, he smiled genially and beckoned
me to come closer, while he continued his ministrations.

My companions and I walked around the huge recumbent
bull, carved directly out of a great natural outcropping of
rock, which occupied the entire center of the temple. It had
been honored by bathing, and the oil and water had splashed
all about. The dark air was heavy with incense and sound
as visitors and worshipers talked, and the priest chanted on.

Standing shoeless on the wet sticky floor, one could not
detach one's self from the scene. It was an experience from
which I could not retreat as a detached observer. I was

there, in it, with my feet pressed to the shoulders of the projecting bedrock from which the huge pagan bull was carved.

Unlike many young people today, I never felt much attraction to Hinduism. Yet the Episcopal Church might indeed be more interesting if our spiritual forebears had prescribed that we remove our shoes. Well, it's just a thought as you take off your shoes after work on a summer afternoon and amble down the path to the pond.

Led by Our Noses

Late summer and autumn have smells not offered to us in winter. There are flowers, of course, and dead leaves, and the distinctive smells of rank weeds. At the seashore there is salty air, and in the country the reassuring and comforting smell of cows.

In the garden there is the peculiar tangy smell of the tomato vine. Maybe it is just one vine, in a pot on the fire escape of a city apartment, but, like a magic carpet, that smell can transport us through time and space to earlier summers, far away on the farm, where roosters greeted the dawn, where the wind rustled in the growing cornstalks, and a heavy dew fell during the cool starlit nights.

Our modern civilization seems to hold an official view of disapproval toward smells. Except for the aroma of flowers, pine trees, and hot coffee, it is assumed that smells are offensive. To say something smells means that it smells bad, unless one quite explicitly adds that it smells good.

According to strict etiquette, even the best of smells are not spoken of. If you go out to a dinner party, and a devastatingly delicious smell is coming from the kitchen, you should not mention it, even if your mouth is convulsively engaged in Pavlovian salivation. Nor should you mention it if your hostess has bedewed herself with a most engaging perfume. As to good smells in church . . . well, some people believe that the only permissible reaction is a severe scowl and a short cough!

116

Why is it acceptable to speak of how things look or sound, but not how they smell? St. Paul was far more matter of fact. "If the whole body were an eye, where would be the hearing? If the whole body were an ear, where would be the sense of smell?" (I Corinthians 12:17). Perhaps we moderns reject our noses precisely because odors do enter into us, they penetrate us as sounds and sights do not. Smells are an affront to that aloofness and independence of the rational intellect which has been the pride of post-renaissance consciousness.

Indeed, the nose links us to an earlier, older, less rational world. Our sense of smell is weaker than that of other mammals, and many smells are but dimly perceived. Yet they powerfully stimulate our imaginations and our memories. The smell of the tomato vine in the summer sun, of the rotten log in the shady forest, of the sidewalk after a summer rain . . . you alone can discover what new or old doors these open for you. In our noses God has given us a mysterious link with the world around us. It can lead us further than we think.

Berchtesgaden

Once when visiting in Germany, I was fortunate to stay several days in a striking locality in the mountains of Bavaria. Down on the floor of the valleys, the ground was bright green with the grass of early spring, and the houses stood together in neat little clusters. Here and there a quaint church stuck up its onion-domed spire. Above the valley, the wooded hillsides ascended, in some places gray, where oaks and other hardwood trees had not yet opened their buds, in other places dark green with a thick covering of spruce and fir. Closer at hand, these seemed like a myriad of Christmas trees standing in the white snow, with their peaks pointing proudly upward. Still higher, steep cliffs of gray rock rose up hundreds of feet, and towering over all the snow-covered peaks mingled with clouds. Ahead of one, to the right, to the left, these majestic peaks met the sky. It was a breathtaking sight.

At night it was equally impressive. Now the houses on the valley floor were represented by little groups of distant lights. The forests were black. The mountain tops loomed up indistinctly in the moonlight. The night sky, which always seems so close overhead in the mountains, positively sparkled with stars, while the waxing moon, like a pale boat, cruised along among them.

This was, to say the least, an inspiring place to be. Here one could not fail to think of the glory of God revealed in his creation. Here one's spirit was lifted up, and one was stirred to aspiration.

118

Yet this was Berchtesgaden! Those of us who are middle-
aged or more know what that name means. How often one
heard of it 45 or 50 years ago! Here Hitler had come to
brood and dream. Here (in the large room where I talked
and laughed with friends in the evening at the hotel) part of
his book *Mein Kampf* was written. Here he had reveled with
his mistress and his cronies. Here he had brought his associates to kindle in them his mad hopes and visions.

The very place that stirred me and many others to an
awareness of the presence of God, had stirred Hitler to
fiendish ambitions and demonic fantasies. The very mountains which I saw as pointing to heaven, he and his associates
saw as pointing to the glory of a conquering Teutonic empire.
All of this really happened, in this very spot.

How could such things be? How could the same landscape have such a strong, but diametrically opposite, effect
on different people? The biblical tradition, the view of the
universe shared by Christians, Jews, and Moslems, gives a
clear answer. There is nothing wrong with the mountains,
stars, or fir trees. The trouble is with human beings. It is in
the human heart that evil has taken root, delivering the
works of God into the power of Satan. We interpret the
world around us, imposing on it our own values and out-
looks. Good things, even the very best things, can be used
for evil purposes. Indeed, perhaps the best things can be used
to accomplish the greatest evil.

Yet I cannot say that natural things are morally neutral.
If one studies the world around us, one cannot fail to find
order, balance, and harmony. These qualities, once we
become conscious of them, are usually perceived as beauty.
When beauty exceeds our own imagination and expectations,
it astonishes us, lifts the mind to a different kind of feeling,
and draws us out of ourselves, as we say. For most people
this is a good experience, an experience that nurtures and
stimulates their sense of values.

Still, what are the values being stimulated? If one's basic and fundamental values are evil, even looking at a beautiful landscape can stimulate wrongdoing. The natural world may point to its Maker, but the pointers can be and often are misunderstood. Without the knowledge of God, the universe is a most dangerous place for human existence.

Law and Life

Is it the way we were created in the first place, or is it the way we fell in the second place, or is it our failure yet to attain our calling in the third place? Why is it that to be a human being is so confoundedly difficult? St. Paul presents it so well in an Epistle for the Third Sunday of Lent: "I do not understand my own actions. For I do not do what I want, but I do the very thing I hate" (Romans 7:15).

Plainly human beings have to have rules. Dogs seem to bury bones automatically, as squirrels do nuts, or as bears and coons put on extra weight for the winter. Yet instinct does not give you or me even the slightest hint as to how to put up a jar of tomatoes or beans for the winter. We have to acquire conscious knowledge, **most** of it transmitted by words, in order to live on this earth. This involves knowledge of things we must do, and things we must not do. Make one little mistake and the tomatoes or the beans may spoil—indeed they may become poisonous.

Most of us can easily follow the line of thought this far. The real problem, unfortunately, is not how to deal with tomatoes or beans. It is how to deal with people (including ourselves). The people who grow and pick tomatoes and beans, who sell them, who buy them, or who eat them—they are the ones to be dealt with, as we find it hard to pay enough, hard to be paid too little, hard to cook for a husband who then says he is too tired to eat, hard to endure a wife who always cooks the same things, hard to love children who

spit out their food . . . and on and on to a whole world of
problems.

For these human problems there are also rules, but we
often do not enjoy obeying them. Ultimately, no amount
of logic, no discussion of ethical values in an agnostic public
school, and no vague secular idealism is going to be much
good if we have the easy opportunity to reach over the fence
into our neighbor's garden, or if we like or dislike his spouse
too much, or if we can misrepresent what we have done to
him by not telling the truth.

It requires not merely laws, but a lawgiver, one who
cannot be evaded or deceived, to direct us into the straight
course. For basic laws that can be counted on our fingers,
the ones Moses gave us still seem to get to the heart of the
matter, and they point to that Lawgiver, whom Moses himself obeyed.

An Ethic of Creation

The doctrine of creation is about God's action in the universe, and it calls for our responding and responsible action in the way we treat the universe and its inhabitants.

All Christian doctrines have some direct or indirect bearing on the whole of life. Yet the doctrine of creation does direct our attention, as most other doctrines do not, specifically toward the physical universe—space and the bodies within it, the earth with its air, water, soil and minerals, and the plant and animal life (including aspects of our own life) which make up the so-called biosphere encompassing the earth's surface. When we speak of the practicality of the doctrine of creation, we are thinking primarily of how this doctrine should affect our practice, our actions, in regard to the inanimate and animate things about us.

It need hardly be said that this raises problems. Ever since, in the third chapter of Genesis, God told Adam to put on his fur coat, take his wife, and go start farming for himself, human beings have had trouble relating themselves to the environment around them. If we wish to look at it this way, human history has been a series of ecological crises. Of course our crisis today is greater: now we really do have the power to make this planet uninhabitable. Yet it is extraordinary what power much smaller numbers of people, in remote periods of history, exercised in enhancing or defacing their environment.

It comes as a surprise to us to reflect that the Bible puts before us, as one of the earliest events in human history, an

environmental crisis which nearly obliterated all terrestrial
life! This was of course the flood (Genesis 6-9). Modern
readers may not interpret it as literal history, but we had
better interpret it as significant history. In this story, man
and beast are doomed because of human sin. Noah, however,
follows God's directions to assume responsibility for the
survival of other living things.

This story must be many thousands of years old, for it is
found, with some variation, in many parts of the world.
What is very notable is that so long ago, when there were far
fewer people on this earth and many more animals, God's
message could be received, that life on this earth is fragile,
and we must accept a major responsibility for its continu-
ance.

The interconnectedness of things, the multitude of causes
that stand behind every event, the balance, order and harmony of the universe, all inspire us with wonder and awe. Yet
it is also mind-boggling. On the one hand, we are challenged
to be good stewards of the universe of which we are part.
On the other hand, the ordinary citizen cannot possibly
formulate sound plans for the ecological welfare of the
environment in which he or she lives. Nor is the average
voter equipped to judge the relative merits of different plans
put forward by experts.

We do not then stop living. As in other complex and
technical areas of life, we can adopt a responsible code of
conduct. It will not solve every problem, but it can at least
keep us moving in the right direction.

Most of us, for example, do not understand all the com-
plexities of business practice. We do believe, however, that
it is in the long run best for all if everyone is honest in
dealing with money—even though dishonesty may, at least in
the short run, be highly advantageous to a few. Financial
honesty is thus canonized as virtuous: dishonesty is under-

stood to be wrong even in cases where it does not appear to hurt others. In short, we accept the authority of ethical precepts governing our conduct in many complex aspects of life. Yet there is no such widespread acceptance of precepts in regard to the "natural" or nonhuman world. It comes as a surprise to learn that the Old Testament, so many centuries ago, not only recognized certain "animal rights" but even rights of the soil and the vegetation (Exodus 20:10, 23:12 and 19, 34:26, Leviticus 25:1-7, and Deuteronomy 5:14, 22:6).

Of course it is always tempting to disobey any rule or ethical directive. Of course we all think our own case is special. The person who drops a paper wrapper in the park wishes to be dispensed because it is so little: the company that dumps a mountain of industrial waste wishes to be dispensed because it is so big! Yet today these things must be taken seriously. There are too many people, too many things, too little time, and too little space. We must recognize, for our own survival, the necessity of ethical standards in dealing with the natural world. This is not just a matter of governmental rules and regulations. It is a matter of ethical norms which we, as people, must accept internally and in the light of our own consciences. Christians, who perceive the power and presence of God in his creation, should be providing leadership that is much needed.

Natural Theology

In a famous scene described in Acts 17 St. Paul, challenged
to give an explanation of his teaching, stands up in the
middle of the Areopagus in Athens, and calls on his hearers
to recognize the existence of the one true God. It is generally supposed that this occurred on the Hill of Ares, the god
of war, located a short distance from the Acropolis. Here,
within sight of the Parthenon and other famous buildings,
an ancient council had customarily held its meetings, and the
modern tourist can visit the hill today.

It has been suggested that in New Testament times this
venerable body normally met somewhere else, taking the
term Areopagus to their new location. In any case, the
apostle was given a most unusual opportunity to address a
prestigious Gentile audience.

He does not begin, as with a Jewish audience, by quoting
the Old Testament or appealing to traditional Hebrew beliefs.
Instead he appropriately appeals to religious practices in
Athens, and to the widespread human experience of life
itself as a gift: God "himself gives to all men life and breath
and everything."

He goes on with two quotations from Greek poets: "In
him we live and move and have our being," and "For we
are indeed his offspring." (The first quotation is sometimes
attributed to Epimenides of the sixth century B.C., and the
second comes from Aratus of the third century B.C.)

All of this is what used to be called "natural theology,"
that is to say, the deducing of an authentic knowledge of

God from the evidence of creation, without recourse to the ancient revelation of God to the Hebrews, or his manifestation of himself in Jesus Christ. Obviously St. Paul found the first article of the Christian faith, belief in God as creator, to be very fundamental.

The apostle also obviously assumed, when Greek pagans spoke seriously about God, as some of their poets and philosophers certainly did, that they, in fact, did mean the God who is God. Our passage states that God has so created people "that they should seek God, in the hope that they might feel after him and find him." This verse is, of course, the basis of our familiar prayer, "O God, who hast made of one blood." Clearly this Gentile effort to "find him" is intended to have some sort of result.

The teaching attributed to St. Paul here in the Book of Acts is fully in accord with what is given in Acts 14:15-17. It also resembles Romans 1:19-23.

In later centuries, the value of natural theology has been questioned, especially by Protestant thinkers. Anglicans and others on the catholic side of the fence have continued to pursue natural theology. This is somewhat ironical, as St. Paul is often considered the fountainhead of Protestantism!

Actually, there are few places in the New Testament which so explicitly indicate that the natural human mind can find God on the basis of natural evidence. On the other hand, the New Testament constantly draws on the experience of this world for figures, analogies, and parables of divine truth.

Such comparisons and figurative expressions are so widespread that if the natural world were destroyed, we would be able to understand very little of the Bible. If the order, beauty, and fruitfulness of nature were obliterated, as through an atomic war, we would have a very difficult time holding any idea of God. The natural world is important to us, not simply as the physical source of food, water, and air, but also as the framework within which people can develop as human beings, as the offspring of God, with hearts and spirits, as well as with bodies and the power of thought.

Spirituality and Creation

Throughout this book we have thought of the doctrine of creation very broadly in terms of the Father, and of the Son, and of the Holy Spirit. This doctrine involves seeing the universe of which we are a part as something made, something fashioned and crafted, by a loving God. It also involves seeing this universe re-defined, re-ordered, and re-directed in Christ. The vision to see this is given to us by the Holy Spirit.

It is not simply a question of how we look at this or that, or of what pleases us, or of what seems most useful or profitable to us. Ultimately we humans must acclimatize ourselves to existence in God's world. This means, along with much else, recognizing values, deep values, even in humble things. It means acknowledging the transcendent aspects of life as those which are most important. In short, in a world made by a loving, purposeful, and personal God, to live a fully human life requires that we have a spirituality.

In many cultures, in many parts of the world and in many periods of history, a tradition of spirituality was taken for granted and a knowledge of it was expected of adult citizens. Today, although we are heirs of two thousand years of Christian life and culture, spirituality is scarcely recognized by most people as being any part of a so-called "normal life."

What is spirituality? Broadly speaking, it is the perception of the spiritual values which bear upon our life, and the development of one's character and personality in ways which reflect and respond to those values. More specifically, a Christian spirituality is the perception of God and an awareness of his presence in all aspects of life, and the conforming of our hearts and minds to Jesus Christ by the power of the Holy Spirit. As it is the created world which surrounds us, and it is through our created senses and faculties that we have knowledge of God, so the ability to perceive spiritual realities in and through their physical manifestations is a basic competence needed by the Christian pilgrim. The knowledge that the Triune God really is in control, this knowledge makes it possible to open our lives to his control and to be nurtured, molded, and brought to maturity in him.

This does not mean a blind, mechanistic obedience or a rigid and impersonal conformity to long sets of rules. Such a view of spirituality would have the effect of dehumanizing us, making us more like animals or machines. On the contrary, the story of creation teaches us to be human, to be men and women who reflect our Maker as we live as persons in community, in harmony with one another and with the world. Indeed we are that unique part of the world which is conscious, which knows God and ourselves and other things.

Catholic Christianity has always recognized and given thanks for the goodness of God as disclosed in creation. We likewise give thanks for our human capacity to perceive at least part of this goodness, to think about it and reflect upon it, and to articulate and share it through words and other forms of expression. Our Catholic Christian heritage affirms and values the fine arts, because this articulation and sharing of beauty is what the painter, poet, musician, architect, or any other kind of artist is trying to do. Art is precisely the way that we lift up the value of things and make it recognizable and communicable. Approached from this direction, we could say that *Christian spirituality is the art of being Christianly human.*

For those who hold the faith of the creeds, a reflective and thoughtful appreciation of the created world is an essential ingredient in such a whole and well-balanced spirituality. We hope and pray that, with the guidance of the Holy Spirit, the suggestions, hints, clues, and guesses which are shared here may contribute to the nurture of such a spirituality in our time.